Cindy

Puppet & Flannelboard
Stories for
Reading Readiness

Editor
Kim Fields

Editor-in-Chief
Sharon Coan, M.S. Ed.

Editorial Project Manager
Mara Ellen Guckian

Illustrators
Blanca Apodaca
Alexandra Artigas
Kevin Barnes

Cover Artist
Brenda DiAntonis

Art Coordinator
Kevin Barnes

Art Director
CJae Froshay

Imaging
James Edward Grace
Rosa C. See
Temo Parra

Product Manager
Phil Garcia

Publishers
Rachelle Cracchiolo, M.S. Ed.
Mary Dupuy Smith, M.S. Ed.

Authors

Belinda Dunnick Karge, Ph.D. and
Marian Meta Dunnick, M.S.

Teacher Created Materials, Inc.
6421 Industry Way
Westminster, CA 92683
www.teachercreated.com
ISBN-0-7439-3701-5
©2003 Teacher Created Materials, Inc.
Made in U.S.A.

Teacher Created Materials

Table of Contents

Introduction. 3

What Is Reading Readiness?. 4

Standards for Language Arts 5

Standards for Mathematics 6

Standards for Science. 7

The ABC's of Storytelling 8

Creating Flannelboards 10

Creating Flannelboard Characters 11

Additional Uses for Patterns 12

Creating Puppets. 13

Ideas for Storage 15

Safety Unit 16

  Meeting the Standards: Safety Unit 17

  Safety Poem 18

    Patterns for Safety Poem 19

  Red Says Stop. 20

    Patterns for Red Says Stop 23

  Traffic Lights 25

    Traffic Lights Coloring. 26

  Red Light—Green Light. 27

  The Traffic Light. 28

  Street Signs 29

All About Me Unit. 31

  Meeting the Standards: Me Unit. 32

  Me Poems 33

  Me Little Me. 34

    Patterns for Me Little Me 36

  Ball for Baby. 39

    Patterns for Ball for Baby. 40

  Body Poems 43

  Here I Am 44

    Patterns for Here I Am 45

  Hello 46

  My Hands 47

  Left and Right Poems 48

Mouse Unit. 49

  Meeting the Standards: Mouse Unit 50

  Five Little Mice 51

    Patterns for Five Little Mice. 52

  My Friend the Mouse 56

  As Small As a Mouse 57

  Timothy Mouse. 58

    Patterns for Timothy Mouse 59

  Great Big Cat and Teeny Little Mouse. 60

    Patterns for Great Big Cat and
    Teeny Little Mouse 61

Dinosaur Unit 62

  Meeting the Standards: Dinosaur Unit 63

  One Dinosaur Went Out to Play 64

    Patterns for One Dinosaur
    Went Out to Play. 65

  Dinosaur History. 68

    Patterns for Dinosaur History 69

  Dinosaurs, Where Are You? 70

    Pattern for Dinosaurs, Where Are You? . . 71

  Dinosaur Poems 72

  Dinosaur Action Poems 73

Space Unit 74

  Meeting the Standards: Space Unit 75

  Rocket Ship. 76

    Patterns for Rocket Ship. 77

  The Little Spaceman Who Listened 79

    Patterns for The Little Spaceman
      Who Listened. 81

  Nine Little Planets 84

    Patterns for Nine Little Planets. 85

  Moon, Sing Me a Song. 86

    Patterns for Moon, Sing Me a Song 87

  Space Helmet 88

  Sleepy Mr. Sun 89

    Patterns for Sleepy Mr. Sun 90

  The Sky Is Full of Clouds. 92

    Patterns for The Sky Is Full of Clouds. . . 93

  Ten Little Martians 94

  Space Poems 95

    Patterns for Space Poems 96

Introduction

Literacy is the key that unlocks all learning. Very young children can be introduced to literacy in a fun, playful way by using finger plays, flannelboard stories, and puppets. The assortment of rhymes, poems, and literature selections provided in this series are research-based and classroom-tested. A variety of suggestions are presented to guarantee the use of standards-based curriculum to assist young learners in exploring basic concepts.

This book is one of three in a series that will introduce educators to ideas for enhancing language experiences, exploring creativity and imagination, and teaching children to enjoy literacy. The materials were compiled to support teachers who may be pressured by the emphasis in education arenas to teach using standards-based criteria and the challenge of how to implement standards-based curriculum in a practical fashion in the classroom.

The Language Arts, Mathematics, and Science Standards for Early Childhood addressed in each section are listed in the beginning of the unit. One or more teaching tips to support the use of the materials accompanies each unit, as does an art activity for expansion of the concept. Ideas for supporting children with special needs and additional enrichment activities round out each unit of stories and patterns.

The activities included in this series are developmentally appropriate practices that support the whole child. The materials presented allow for kinesthetic (tactile), auditory, vocal, and visual stimulation. The mastery of oral language is a prerequisite to effective emergent literacy. Children learn about the relationship between spoken and written language as they hear, tell, and retell stories. They begin to understand how to create a story sequence with a beginning, a middle, and an end. Children orally practice behaviors that will later be critical to learning to read (the link between pictures and words) and to write (the ability to say it, sequence it, and show it in print).

The suggested flannelboard stories and puppets are enticing visual and tactile aids that make learning a hands-on experience. By watching and then manipulating the puppets, children will solidify concepts while improving their motor skills. Puppets allow the young child a safe place to experience the world of imagination. Sometimes a shy child will speak to a puppet before speaking to an adult. Positive self-esteem is strengthened when children have the opportunity to successfully manipulate the puppet and tell the story themselves. The initial time spent creating these materials is well worth the effort, not to mention the fun! The patterns are versatile and can be used in different stories. Enlarging each of the stories to display for the children is a critical component of a reading readiness program. This leads children to recognize that a story consists of many individual words.

Reading readiness concepts including oral language, predictable stories, and repetitive rhymes are presented in this book through a variety of literature selections. Simple, easy-to-make puppets and related activities accompany each unit. Young learners are introduced to the world of literacy by memorizing the different pieces of selected literature and acting them out with a teacher. Children learn to use words and their functions. Later, they can reinforce what they have learned by using the puppets to retell the stories amongst themselves.

The standards for Language Arts, Mathematics, and Science listed on pages 5–7 are met with the activities in *Puppets & Flannelboard Stories for Reading Readiness*. These compilations of standards and objectives are similar to the ones required by your school district. The pages can be posted in the classroom for reference when planning lessons and for parent information. Family members are often surprised at the amount of "learning" inherent in storytelling.

Every attempt has been made to give credit to the authors of individual stories, though many have been passed down through oral tradition. We apologize for any original sources we are unable to identify.

What Is Reading Readiness?

Literacy development begins prior to the knowledge of the alphabet and formal reading instruction. *Starting Out Right: A Guide to Promoting Children's Reading Success,* published by the National Research Council (1999), provides specific recommendations from America's leading researchers on how to help children become successful readers. They recommend that a high-quality preschool include many opportunities for language development. One of the best ways to enhance language is to provide materials that are of high interest to the child, are easy to remember (i.e., repetition), and promote avenues for questions (i.e., what happened first, second, etc., or what if we changed the ending of the story?).

Children benefit from hearing simple stories they can relate to their own experiences. For example, in the Safety Unit, children are introduced to the traffic light and what its colors mean. They can, in turn, look for traffic lights in their own neighborhoods and relate the words in the rhymes to their personal experiences. The National Association for the Education of Young Children refers to this as learning information in a meaningful context and considers it essential for children's understanding and development of reading.

This book contains many predictable stories. The repetitive rhymes and rhythms will provide for full participation and autonomy of action that your children can enjoy. Learning that storytelling leads to enjoyment provides motivation for young children to learn to read. Thus, developmentally appropriate reading readiness activities can be the key to a successful reading experience in elementary school.

The book, *Puppets & Flannelboard Stories for Reading Readiness*, provides the educator with several thematic units. The themes were carefully selected because they are high-interest items for young children. Each unit includes several stories. Young children demonstrate a variety of ways that they understand a story. You will delight in watching your children laugh, smile, relate to an object or action, perform an action that is shown or mentioned in the story, and make associations across stories. These are all reading-readiness skills.

It is suggested that the teacher create a thematic book for each unit. Keep several copies in the classroom and send the stories home for the children to "read" to their families. A critical component in reading readiness is when a child wants to move his or her finger or whole hand across a line of print and "read" what it says. (The rendition may be the exact text or an accurate paraphrase.) Adults are often fascinated that a young child can recite whole phrases from a favorite story.

Considerable print exists in a child's world. As children are closer to beginning to read (emergent literacy), they will recognize that printed words have a different function than the pictures. As a child hears the variety of stories, rhymes, and rhythms in these thematic units, he or she will learn to explore and understand the sequence of a story. The research in the field of reading tells us that children's readiness experiences play a key role in the learning and development of reading.

For more information, refer to *Developmentally Appropriate Practice in Early Childhood Programs* by Sue Bredekamp. (NAEYC), 1997.

Standards for Language Arts

- ❑ Asks and answers questions
- ❑ Comprehends what others are saying
- ❑ Demonstrates competency in speaking as a tool for learning
- ❑ Demonstrates competency in listening as a tool for learning
- ❑ Follows simple directions
- ❑ Identifies and sorts common words into basic categories
- ❑ Identifies characters, settings, and important events
- ❑ Is developing fine motor skills
- ❑ Listens
- ❑ Produces meaningful linguistic sounds
- ❑ Produces rhyming words in response to an oral prompt
- ❑ Recites familiar stories and rhymes with patterns
- ❑ Recites short stories
- ❑ Recognizes colors
- ❑ Recognizes color and shape words
- ❑ Recognizes meaningful words
- ❑ Responds to oral directions
- ❑ Responds to oral questions
- ❑ Retells familiar stories
- ❑ Auditorily tracks each word in a sentence
- ❑ Understands that printed material provides information
- ❑ Uses picture clues to aid comprehension
- ❑ Uses picture clues to make predictions about content

The standards above are a compilation from the National Association for the Education of Young Children, the National English Language Standards for Public Schools, and the National Standards of English Language Arts.

Standards for Mathematics

- ☐ Conceptualizes one-to-one correspondence
- ☐ Divides objects into categories
- ☐ Compares whole numbers
- ☐ Connects math with the real world
- ☐ Connects math with other disciplines
- ☐ Copies and extends patterns
- ☐ Counts to ten
- ☐ Describes basic shapes
- ☐ Estimates quantities
- ☐ Explores activities involving chance
- ☐ Identifies equal/unequal portions
- ☐ Identifies shapes in the real world
- ☐ Identifies shapes in different positions
- ☐ Implements a problem-solving strategy
- ☐ Learns number names
- ☐ Learns number symbols
- ☐ Makes predictions
- ☐ Names basic shapes
- ☐ Recognizes and collects data
- ☐ Reads whole numbers to ten
- ☐ Solves simple equations
- ☐ Sorts basic shapes
- ☐ Uses verbal communication
- ☐ Uses pictorial communication
- ☐ Uses symbolic communication
- ☐ Understands the problem
- ☐ Classifies objects

The standards above are a compilation from the National Association for the Education of Young Children, and the National Council of Teachers of Mathematics.

Standards for Science

- ☐ Applies problem-solving skills
- ☐ Classifies
- ☐ Communicates
- ☐ Discusses changes in seasons
- ☐ Explores animals
- ☐ Explores reptiles
- ☐ Identifies body parts and the five senses
- ☐ Identifies color in the real world
- ☐ Identifies objects by color
- ☐ Identifies objects by properties
- ☐ Identifies objects by shape
- ☐ Identifies objects by size
- ☐ Observes, identifies, and measures objects
- ☐ Predicts
- ☐ Problem-solves through group activities
- ☐ Recognizes opposites

The standards above are a compilation from the National Association for the Education of Young Children and the National Science Foundation (NSF).

The ABC's of Storytelling

Adapt the story for your group. Shorten, expand, or change the wording for different age levels. The attention span of young children can vary tremendously.

Be creative with ways to enhance involvement and promote active participation. For example, ask everyone to clap when they hear a certain word.

Check for understanding, monitor and adjust learning as you watch, and listen to your students. Use children's names and tell children what they did. For example, "That is correct, Juan. You knew it was a blue square."

Devote time to preparation. Make certain you know the story and have all the follow-up materials ready. Accentuate the plot and characters.

Emphasize the incidents that appeal to children. For example, the element of surprise can create vehicles for application in the real world. Use real-life examples and pictures when available.

Frequently ask children to respond. Ask them to repeat a line or give you a similar word. Plan ways to reinforce basic language principles.

Gain children's attention prior to beginning the story. For example, sing a favorite song everyday. The consistency and structure will help remind the children that it is time for storytime.

Hold the book so that the children can see, or point to, the figures on the flannelboard.

Individualize your instruction. Think about each child in your group and choose stories that align with his or her likes and interests.

Justify literacy! Send home notes to parents letting them know the book, story, or poem you are teaching. Ask them for support at home. Encourage parents to reread the story at home for reinforcement.

Knowledge of the early childhood standards will enhance your teaching. Review the charts provided in this book and integrate these standards into your lesson plans.

List the key concepts for a story, and repeat the learning throughout storytime. Make lesson planning a valuable component of your program. Keep the key concept lists and plan to spiral back to them to reinforce concepts.

Materials should be age appropriate. Use the teaching tips and expansion activities for children with special needs or those in need of enrichment.

The ABC's of Storytelling (cont.)

New books are wonderful, but the old favorites are just as grand! Use a variety of titles in your classroom.

Open, body, close should be the sequence of every storytime. Open with an attention-getter. Preview the activity, follow with the body of the story, and close with some type of review or follow-up activity.

Pacing is critical. Check yourself during the lesson: Am I moving too quickly, too slowly? If the children are restless, change the pace or try a different activity.

Question the children. Ask focused questions like "What else works like this?" Ask the children to repeat/retell the story. Ask, "How do you think the story will end?" Ask, "Do you know what will happen next?" Use eye contact and affirm the children's answers.

Repeat favorites; children learn through repetition. Reread or retell the story many, many times.

Sit in close proximity, at the level of the children whenever possible. Providing a set structure for circle time supports learning. Sit in the same place, always begin with a familiar opening transition song, etc.

Treasure teachable moments. If a child wants to relate the story to his or her own life (maybe he or she has the same breed of animal as in the story) allow the time, and use it as a teachable opportunity.

Utilize all available space, both in the area you are telling the story and on the flannelboard (if using a flannelboard).

Vary your facial expression and use your voice as a tool. You may want to whisper to emphasize a special part of the story.

Words you use should be clear and simple. Enunciate and speak slowly.

X-ray vision—Use eye contact as an antecedent to prevent unacceptable behavior.

Your attitude is contagious! If you have fun and enjoy storytime, so will the children with whom you work.

ZZZZZZZZZZZZ-end. Emphasize the end of the story and draw closure to the lesson with follow-up and/or extension activities. This will help children remember the story and concepts covered. When they arrive home and a parent asks, "What did you learn in school today?", they are more likely to recall the story and concepts learned if there has been closure to the lesson.

Creating Flannelboards

There are many flannelboards on the market, however sometimes creating your own is more appealing. You know what size and shape your classroom can accommodate. Cut a large piece of corrugated cardboard to the size you wish to create a flannelboard. Cut a piece of felt 1" (2.54 cm) larger than the cardboard. Cover the cardboard with the felt, taping the overlap in the back. (Note: Light blue makes a good background, since sky is often a good backdrop. A black background, on the other hand, can be quite striking.) Consider the following ideas when designing your own flannelboard.

Free-Standing/Tabletop Board

Easel Flannelboard

Pocket-Chart Board

Felt Apron

Creating Flannelboard Characters

Flannelboard characters are inexpensive to make and provide wonderful visuals for young learners. The patterns provided in this book can be made with felt or other materials, and assembled with standard glue or a glue gun. Some require simple sewing. All patterns can be enhanced with decorations. Use your imagination. Incorporate your own ideas and those of the children to construct personalized teaching tools for your own classroom.

Cut the original patterns out of heavy cardstock or cardboard and laminate them. These patterns should be saved in a central file area or in the same container as the figures and the story. This way, if one is lost or ruined it is simple to replace.

Tips for Enhancing Flannelboard Pieces

1. Use scissors with different edges when cutting out paper pieces to be attached to felt backing. Many styles are sold in craft, hobby, and fabric stores. Some have rounded edges, some are scalloped, and some have zigzag edges. Pinking shears are fun too, and they work on fabric!

2. Keep leftover scraps of felt and fabric from other projects. You never know when a small piece will come in handy as a decoration, an eye, or a clothing detail.

3. Collect scraps of ribbon, bows, trim, and buttons.

4. Use leftover glitter and sequins for special details. Glitter glue and puff paints are handy as well. Consider using them when creating royal characters or when adding scales to a fish.

5. Yarn and curling ribbon make great hair.

6. Attach a small piece of Velcro® or felt to the back of most small puppets for use on the flannelboard.

7. Cut out characters from old storybooks and magazines. Attach them to felt with glue. Use these just as you would a felt piece.

Additional Uses for Patterns

The patterns included in this book are quite versatile and simple to use. The more you work with them, the more uses you will discover for them.

- Reproduce the patterns on construction paper, and provide the children with materials to color, cut out, and glue the pieces together. Then they can have a set of figures for each story to take home and practice with parents or other family members.

- Use the patterns to create story mobiles and hang them from the ceiling.

- Magnetic strips can be glued to the backs of some flannel pieces for use on a magnetic board.

- Use the patterns as placeholders on the classroom calendar.

- Use the patterns to create an individual big book as a keepsake for each child in the class. For each book, cut two pieces of poster board to the desired size. Glue the pattern and copy of the story onto each of the pages. Be sure to make an extra book for your reading corner or reading station!

- Children love to tell and retell stories. Consider making a second set of patterns for each story. The duplicate pieces can be kept in the children's story area. Allow children to mix and match the pieces to create new stories, or to retell variations of the favorites you have shared with them.

Additional Resources

Gould, Patti and Joyce Sullivan. *The Inclusive Early Childhood Classroom: Easy Ways to Adapt Learning Centers for ALL Children.* Gryphon House Publishers, 1999.

This book offers a variety of excellent strategies designed to adapt curriculum centers for children with special needs.

Sandall, Susan and Ilene Schwartz. *Building Blocks for Teaching Preschoolers with Special Needs.* Paul H. Brooks Publishing Company, 2002.

The authors provide many creative ideas for curriculum modifications, teaching and embedding learning opportunities, and child-focused instructional strategies for children.

Puppets and Flannelboard Sets

Artfelt 1102 N. Brand Blvd. San Fernando, CA 91340 (818) 365-1021

E-mail: artfelt@mail.com

Artfelt offers a wide selection of products. Their quality finger and hand puppets are designed to also work on felt boards, bulletin boards and pocket charts.

Creating Puppets

There are many materials you can use to create puppets. Below you will find five different types of puppets and directions for their creation. Some will incorporate the patterns supplied in this book, and others can be made easily with household or classroom items.

Stick Puppets

Patterns for stick puppets can be copied onto heavy cardstock or cardboard, cut out, and decorated. Some teachers like to laminate the pieces. The cutouts can then be attached to craft sticks, tongue depressors, paint stirrers, or yardsticks for easy accessibility.

Mini stick puppets can be made by attaching stickers to craft sticks.

Don't forget about wooden spoons. Faces can be drawn or glued onto them to create almost instant puppets.

Note: When telling the story, whoever is designated to hold the puppet holds onto the item (type of stick) to which the pattern was attached.

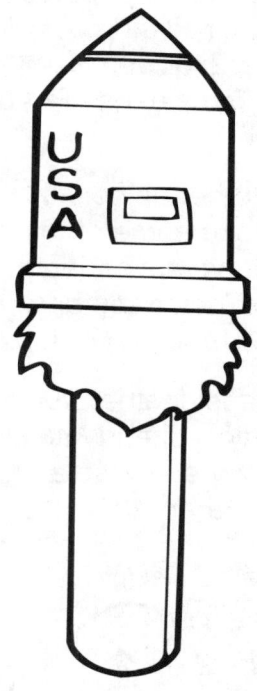

Pop-Up Puppets

The element of surprise is a valuable attention-getting device in the early childhood classroom. Use a cylinder (paper tube), coffee can, Styrofoam® cup, or paper cup for the base of the pop-up puppets.

Poke a hole in the center of the base and insert a craft stick, sturdy straw, or dowel. Attach an old doll head (or a head created from a Styrofoam ball wrapped with yarn or covered with nylons) to the dowel.

Use a glue gun to attach the head to the dowel if the dowel cannot be pushed into the head. For added interest, decorate the handmade head with yarn, fabric, etc.

Creating Puppets *(cont.)*

Hand Puppets

Use old gloves to create puppets for the number stories. Attach a small strip of Velcro® with a glue gun to each finger of the glove. Use the glove puppet when introducing counting stories. Put one finger puppet on each glove finger.

There are many other objects that can be used for hand puppets. If you take some of the stuffing out of a stuffed animal, you will have a wonderful puppet. It is best to remove the stuffing from a slit in the back or the bottom of the animal. Leave the head, arms, and/or legs filled.

Mittens, paper bags, feather dusters, socks, a Slinky®, shirt sleeves, rubber gloves, and kitchen hot pads can all be used to create hand puppets. Use a variety of materials to create the faces of the characters in the story you are telling.

Face Puppets

A face puppet can be created on a paper plate, dust pan, sponge, Ping-Pong paddle, fly swatter, paintbrush, or wooden spoon. Decorate the face to match the characters or animals in the corresponding story.

Finger Puppets

Simple, one-time-only, finger puppets can be made by covering a child's fingertips with masking tape or stickers. Faces can be drawn on the tape or plain stickers. Seasonal stickers, such as pumpkins, can also be used for specific stories or songs.

To make a more permanent puppet, glue felt pieces or pictures to a film canister or cut off the fingers of old gloves and decorate them with a permanent marker or felt details.

Finger puppets can also be made by cutting out two small, identical pattern pieces and gluing them together, leaving a small opening at the base for a finger to fit in. Any puppet small enough to fit on a glove will work for a finger puppet.

Ideas for Storage

There are many ways to store puppets and felt pieces. Try to keep all of the characters for one story in the same container. Always include a copy of the story. This organizational method can come in handy for people who do not memorize the stories and need the written words or prompts. Consider, too, adding a list of the required props on the container. This is especially useful when some of the props used are from other stories or are materials used in other areas of the classroom.

Storage options include the following ideas:

Tape a file folder together on two sides and staple string to the top for a handle. Attach the story or write its title on the outside of the folder. List the props on the other side of the folder.

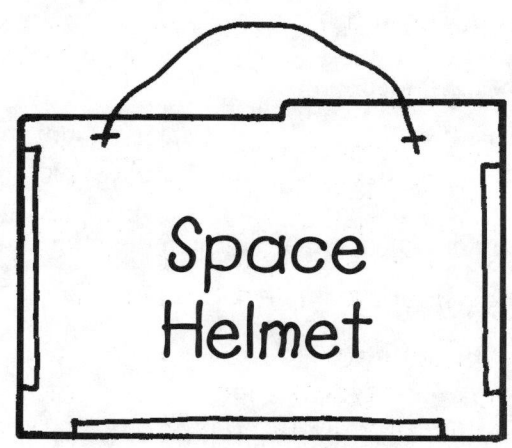

Label a gallon-size, plastic resealable bag with the title of the story. Enclose a copy of the story and the puppet pieces. Consider attaching a three-ring strip to each bag. The felt figures and the corresponding stories can then be stored in a large three-ring binder for easy access.

Collect new pizza boxes (many shops will gladly donate them to schools). Attach the story to the lid and place the pieces inside. If you plan to stack these boxes, it is a good idea to label the side of the box as well.

Create a storage container out of a shoebox. Add a copy of the story. Laminate it if possible. List the contents of the box on the inside top of the lid.

Safety Unit

This unit is focused on one specific area of safety, street signs. These are important, real-world symbols that all children must learn early in their lives. Different stories and finger plays are introduced to increase awareness of these signs. Young children will learn what a traffic light looks like, what the colors on it represent, and most importantly, what to do at a traffic light! The last pages of the section include a variety of street signs to review with students.

Teaching Tip

The focus of this unit is on the Safety Poem (page 18) and its meaning. Be certain to really emphasize the three colors in the traffic light. After you have introduced all the stories and poems, ask the children to retell them, making certain they focus on the colors. Have different sizes of red, yellow, and green circles available. Encourage the students to use the circles in their own safety storytelling.

Art Activity

Colored Play Dough

Ingredients for each color:

3 cups flour (additional flour for kneading)

powdered drink mix (you will need a packet of red, yellow, and green)

2 cups boiling water

3 tablespoons vegetable oil

½ cup salt

Directions:

1. Combine flour and the red powdered drink mix in a bowl. Pour in boiling water.
2. Add oil and salt to mixture and let it cool.
3. Knead the dough using additional flour if necessary.
4. Repeat the process to make yellow dough and again for green dough.
5. Store in separate, closed containers overnight.

To assemble the traffic light, assist each child in making three play dough balls. Have each child smash the balls on a black sheet of precut construction paper, using the rectangle pattern on page 19. Allow the project to dry. Glue the balls to the construction paper using a glue stick.

Supporting Children with Special Needs

Structure is critical to children with special needs. They may find it challenging to be using the same traffic light for five different poems. Recite the "Safety Poem" every day the unit is discussed. This will reinforce the poem and allow for the required structure. The "Safety Poem" is a wonderful way to begin circle time or to transition to outdoor play. You might even consider developing a large traffic light to use as part of your classroom management system. Put a marker of some sort on the appropriate color. You could mark green to go outside or red to stop working and clean up. These small connections will be appreciated by the learners with special needs.

Enrichment

Have children take a safety walk around the school and neighborhood. Say the "Safety Poem" at each traffic light. Note other signs along the way. Have children create their own representative safety poems as they learn about other safety issues—fire, earthquake, etc.

Meeting the Standards: Safety Unit

Language Arts

- Comprehends what others are saying
- Demonstrates competency in speaking as a tool for learning
- Demonstrates competency in listening as a tool for learning
- Follows simple directions
- Identifies and sorts common color words into basic categories
- Listens
- Produces rhyming words in response to an oral prompt
- Recites familiar stories and rhymes with patterns
- Recites short stories
- Recognizes colors
- Responds to oral directions
- Responds to oral questions
- Retells familiar stories
- Understands that printed material provides information
- Uses picture clues to aid comprehension
- Uses picture clues to make predictions about content

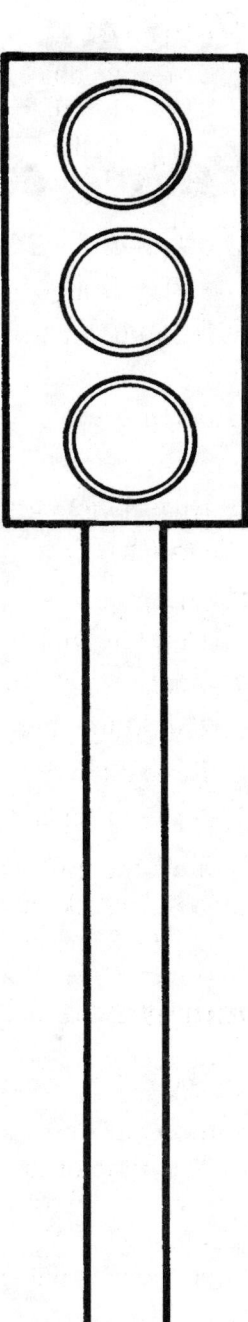

Mathematics

- Conceptualizes one-to-one correspondences
- Connects math with other disciplines
- Copies and extends patterns
- Identifies shapes in the real world
- Uses pictorial communication
- Uses symbolic communication

Science

- Classifies
- Communicates
- Identifies objects by color and shape
- Identifies color in the real world
- Observes, identifies, and measures objects
- Predicts
- Problem-solves through group activities

Safety Poem

(Begin by placing the black rectangle on the flannelboard.)

Red on top, and green below.

(Put the red circle at the top of the black rectangle and the green circle at the bottom.)

Red says, "Stop," and green says, "Go!"

(Point to the red and green circles.)

Yellow says, "Wait," even if you're late.

(Place the yellow circle in the middle of the other two circles on the flannelboard.)

Patterns for Safety Poem

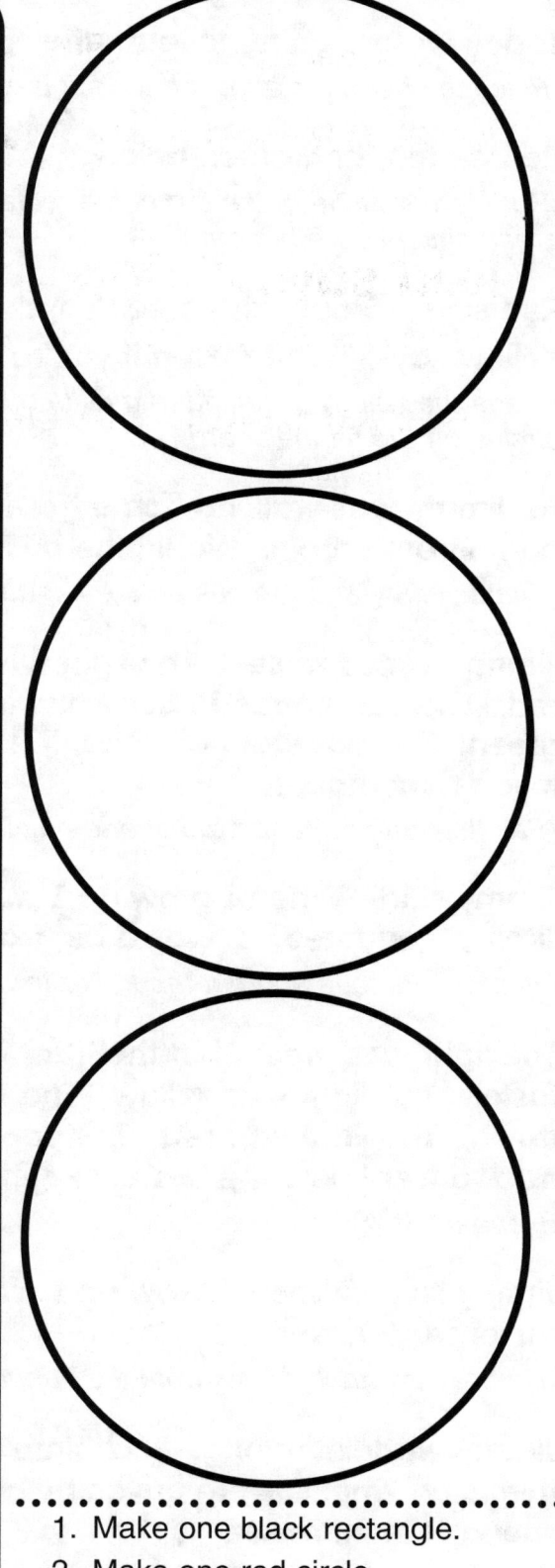

1. Make one black rectangle.
2. Make one red circle.
3. Make one yellow circle.
4. Make one green circle.

Red Says Stop

Today we are going to learn the "Safety Poem."

(Place the black rectangle on the flannelboard. Have the red, yellow, and green circles ready.)

Red on top, and green below.

(Put the red circle at the top of the rectangle and the green circle at the bottom.)

Red says, "Stop," and green says, "Go."
Yellow says, "Wait," even if you're late.

(Place the yellow circle in the middle of the other two circles on the flannelboard.)

As Jimmy was walking home from school, he saw a bus carrying other children home from school. Would the bus driver know the poem?

(Place Jimmy and the bus on the flannelboard.)

Jimmy waited to see. The light was yellow. The bus slowed down. The light was red. The bus stopped. Someone in the bus waved to Jimmy. The light turned green. The bus went on. Yes, the bus driver knew the "Safety Poem." Let's see if you remember it.

(Say the "Safety Poem" together as a class.)

Jimmy said, "When I grow up I want to drive a bus." Well, what is coming now? Jimmy wondered. It was a big trailer truck.

(Remove the bus and put the trailer truck on the flannelboard.)

The light was green, but the truck did not go faster. The light was yellow. The truck slowed down. The light was red. It stopped. Yes, the truck driver knew the "Safety Poem."

(Repeat the "Safety Poem.")

Jimmy said, "When I grow up I want to be a trailer truck driver."

(Remove the trailer truck from the flannelboard.)

Jimmy waddled along. Each time he came to a traffic light he watched to see if things on wheels were driven by people who knew what to do. All at once, he saw a cement mixer.

(Put the cement mixer on the flannelboard.)

Red Says Stop *(cont.)*

"Oh, dear," said Jimmy. "That cement mixer is awfully big. Maybe the driver can't see the traffic light." But the cement mixer stopped when the light was red. The cement mixer driver also knew the "Safety Poem."

(Repeat the "Safety Poem.")

Jimmy said, "When I grow up I want to be a cement mixer driver."

(Remove the cement mixer from the flannelboard.)

Next a pickup came along carrying vegetables to market.

(Put the pickup on the flannelboard.)

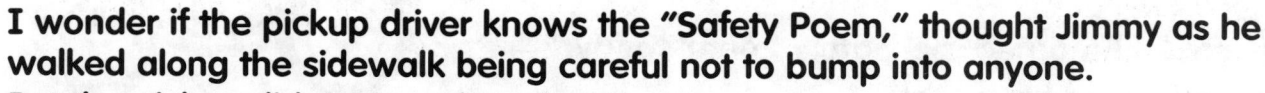

I wonder if the pickup driver knows the "Safety Poem," thought Jimmy as he walked along the sidewalk being careful not to bump into anyone.
But the pickup didn't even slow down!
Do you know why?
Yes, the light was green.

(Repeat the "Safety Poem.")

Jimmy said, "When I grow up I want to be a pickup truck driver."

(Remove the pickup from the flannelboard.)

Along came a motorcycle driver.

(Put the police motorcycle on the flannelboard.)

Maybe she didn't know the traffic rules. Of course she did.
The driver was a police officer, and she was particularly careful.
Jimmy said the "Safety Poem" to himself as he walked along.

(Repeat the "Safety Poem.")

Jimmy said, "When I grow up I want to be a motorcycle driver."

(Remove the police motorcycle from the flannelboard.)

"Whiz!" A small car came along going too fast.

(Quickly move the car onto the flannelboard.)

The light turned red, but the car was going too fast to stop.
"Screech!" A car going the other way had to put on its brakes very quickly.

(Make a siren sound.)

A siren! Was there a fire? No.

(Make a siren sound.)

Was it a police motorcycle? Yes.

(Put the police motorcycle on the flannelboard.)

Red Says Stop *(cont.)*

"Someone is going to get a ticket," said Jimmy sadly.

"I guess he never learned the 'Safety Poem.'"

But you and I know that the car driver did know the safety rules.

He just didn't think.

The police officer gave the driver a ticket so that
he will remember next time.

(Remove the car and the police motorcycle from the flannelboard.)

By now Jimmy was home.

His mother gave him a kiss and a big hug.

(Put Mother next to Jimmy on the flannelboard.)

Jimmy said, "I learned the 'Safety Poem' today."

And he said it for his mother.

Maybe you can say the "Safety Poem" for your father or mother
when he or she comes and picks you up. Shall we see?

(Repeat the "Safety Poem.")

Jimmy   **Mother**

Use the patterns above and on pages 19, 23, and 24 to create the traffic light, Jimmy, Mother,
car, trailer truck, bus, pickup, cement mixer, and police motorcycle flannel pieces.

Teacher Suggestion: Substitute toy vehicles for those mentioned in the story.

Patterns for Red Says Stop

1. Make one car.
2. Make one trailer truck.
3. Make one bus.

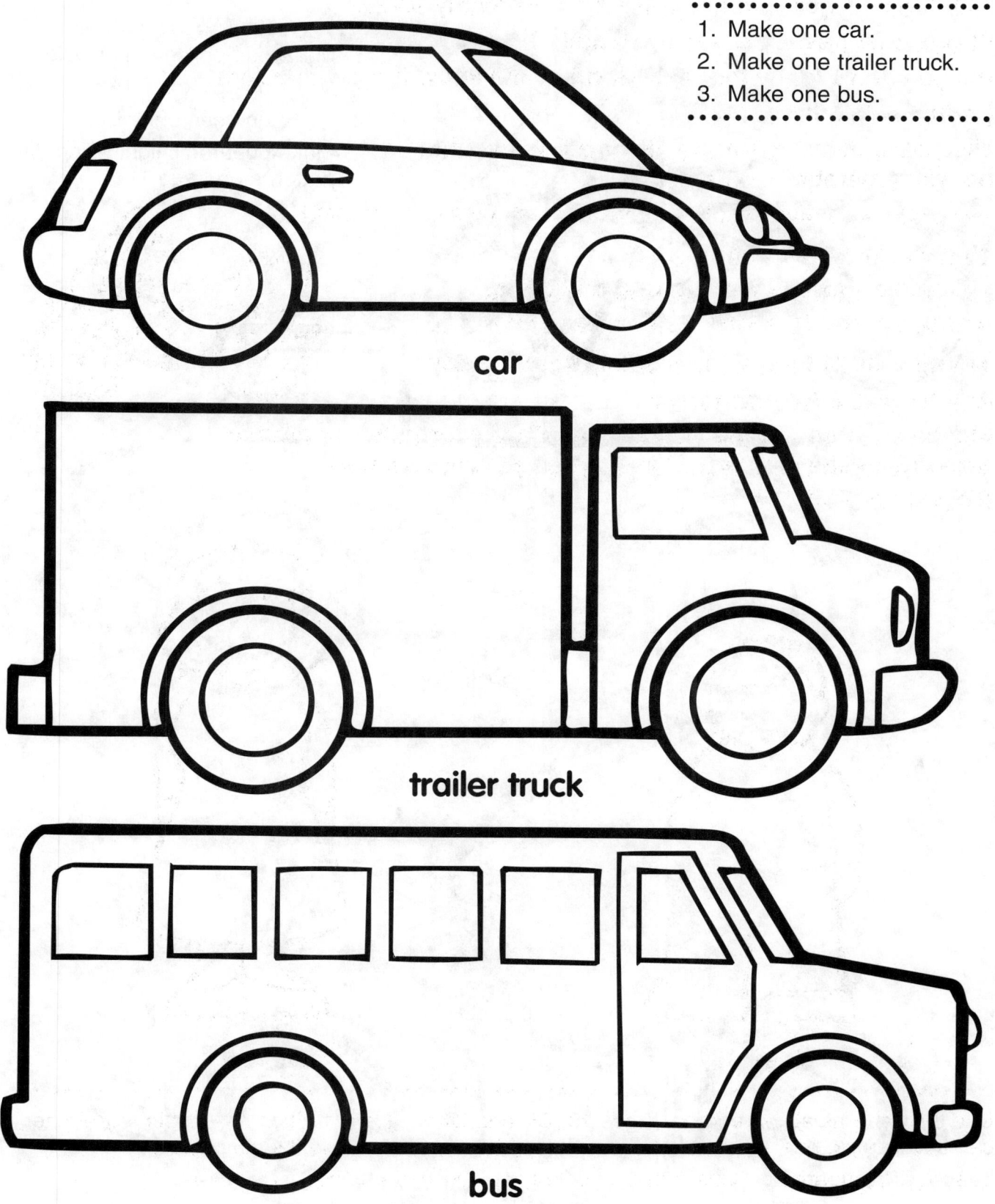

car

trailer truck

bus

Patterns for Red Says Stop *(cont.)*

1. Make one police motorcycle.
2. Make one pickup.
3. Make one cement mixer.
4. Make one traffic light using the patterns on page 19.

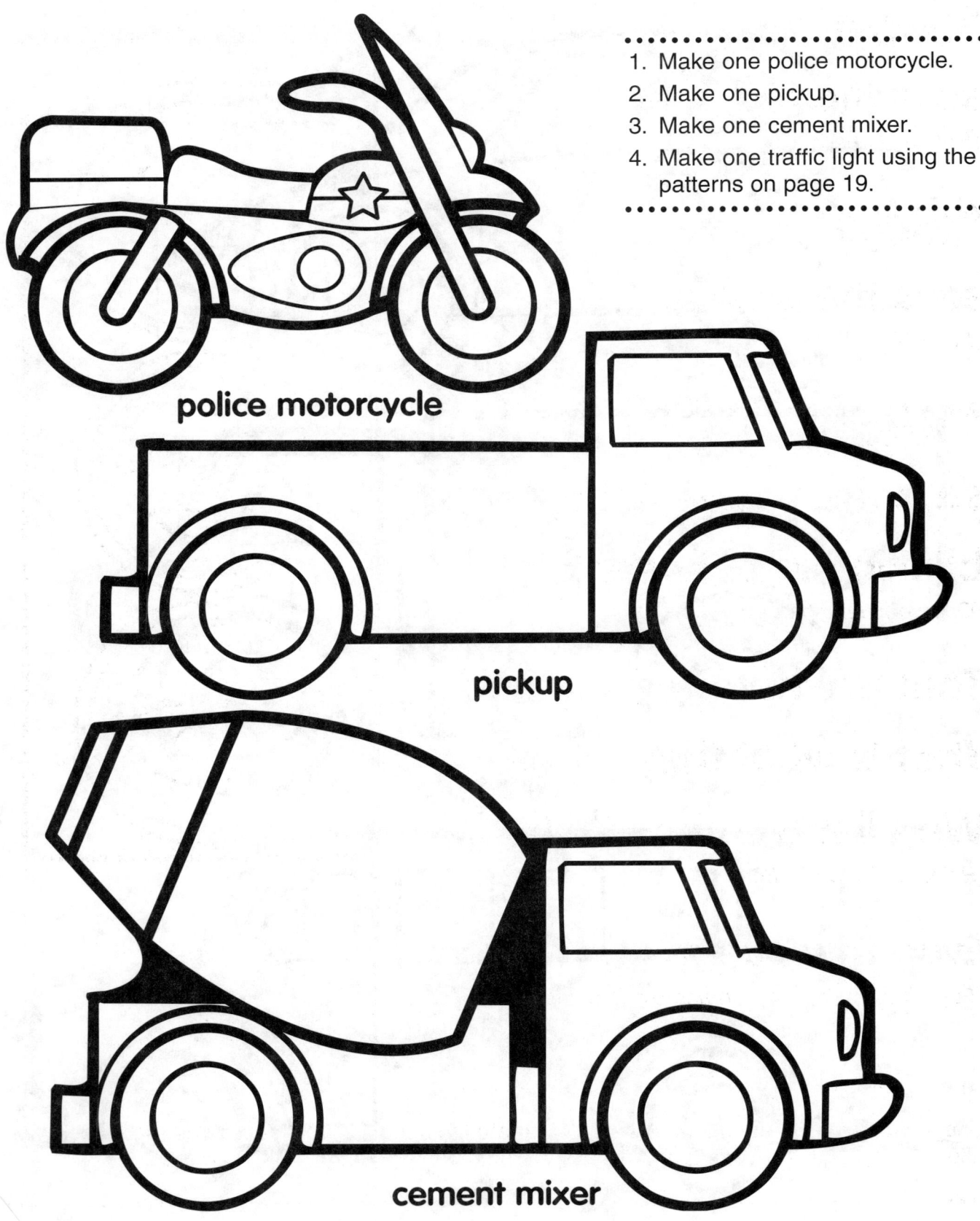

police motorcycle

pickup

cement mixer

24

Traffic Lights

"Stop,"

says the red light.
(Hold up hand.)

"Go,"

says the green.
(Point finger.)

"Wait,"

says the yellow light,

blinking in between.
(Open and shut hand.)

That is what they say and

That is what they mean.

We all must obey them,
(Point to all the children.)

Even the Queen!
(Form hands into a crown and place on head.)

....

Use the traffic light patterns on page 19 to create the traffic light flannel pieces. As a review, offer the students the opportunity to color the traffic light on page 26.

....

Traffic Lights Coloring *(cont.)*

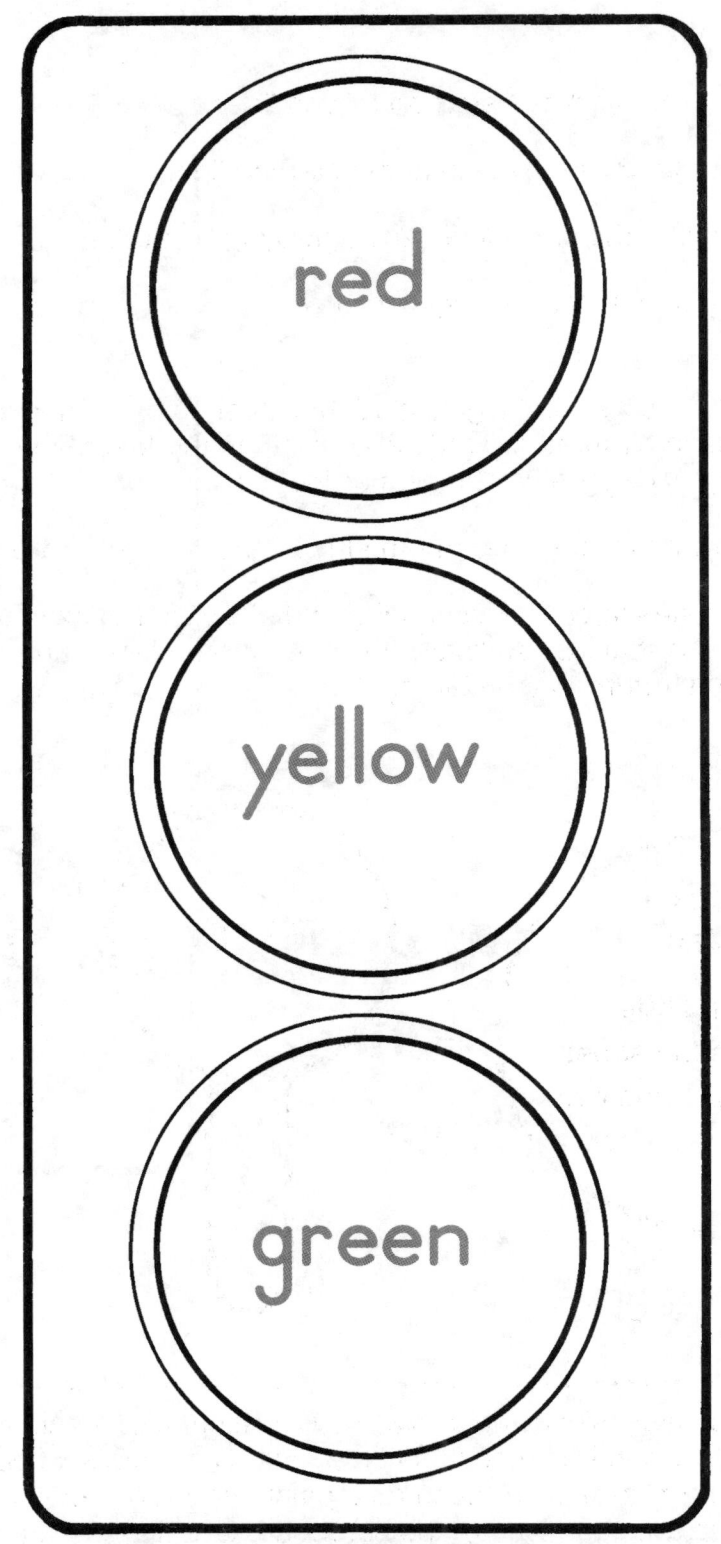

Directions: Color the traffic light and trace the color words.

26

Red Light–Green Light

This activity is best played outdoors. You may wish to start with the poem given below.

Directions

1. Use cones or chalk to mark the start and finish lines.

2. Have all students stand side by side at the starting line.

3. The teacher stands at the finish line, facing away from students.

4. When the teacher shouts "Green Light," students may either walk or run toward the finish line.

5. When the teacher shouts "Red Light," students must stop. Immediately after shouting "Red Light," the teacher turns around. Any students the teacher sees moving after shouting "Red Light" must return to the starting line.

6. Then the teacher turns facing away from students and shouts "Green Light" once again.

7. The teacher continues to call "Green Light" and "Red Light" until one student crosses the finish line. Then it is that student's turn to shout "Green Light" and "Red Light," and the rest of the students return to the starting line.

Stop, Look, and Listen

Stop, look, and listen
When you cross the street.
First use your eyes and ears
And then use your feet.

You may wish to use a visual signal when playing Red Light–Green Light. Cut a large red circle and a large green circle from construction paper. Cut a piece of cardboard the same size as the circles. Glue a large stick, such as a paint stirrer or a ruler, onto the cardboard. Then glue the red circle onto one side of the cardboard and the green circle onto the other side. Now students can see the color that is called while hearing its name and viewing the color word.

The Traffic Light

(Sing to the tune of "The Wheels on the Bus.")

The traffic light goes blink, blink, blink,

Blink, blink, blink, blink, blink, blink.

You should stop and think, think, think,

Before you cross the street.

The traffic light glows red, red, red,

Red, red, red, red, red, red.

This means stop and wait, wait, wait,

Before you cross the street.

The traffic light glows green, green, green

Green, green, green, green, green, green.

This means go so walk, walk, walk.

Walk across the street.

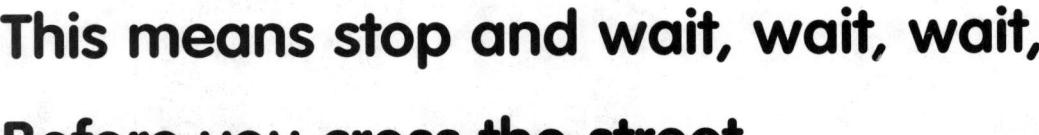

Have students hold up red and green circles at the appropriate times during the song. Role-play crossing the street safely. Stress to children that they should always look left, then right, then left again before crossing any street.

Street Signs

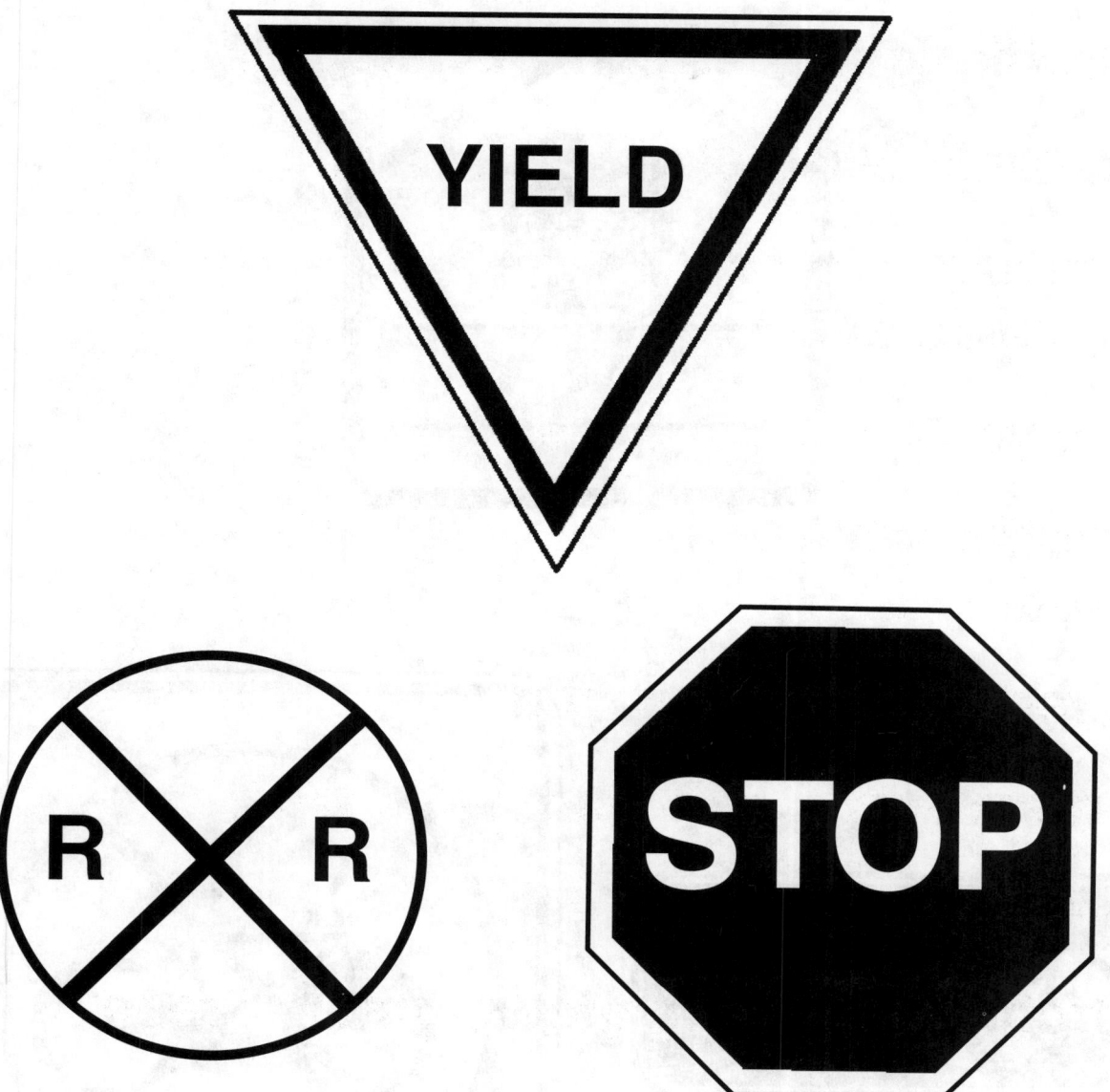

Explore street signs in your area once children are familiar with the traffic light.

1. Cut out the cards above and on page 30. Enlarge if possible and attach each sign to a paint stirrer or craft stick.

2. Introduce each sign and explain its meaning. Discuss the actual colors of the sign.

3. Review as needed.

Street Signs *(cont.)*

....

Use masking tape to create streets. Add a crosswalk at one end. Enlarge the street signs above and on page 29 and place them in the appropriate places along the streets. Have children role-play different street safety rules.

....

All About Me Unit

Children need to feel good about themselves if they are to be socially competent. The art of interacting with other children in a socially acceptable way is a prerequisite for other skills. Talking about "me" encourages children and improves their self-esteem. Introducing poems related to body parts, sounds, and the directions left and right provides an excellent forum for children to learn critical reading readiness skills.

Teaching Tips

Once children know who they are, they can move toward other social skills such as sharing. Remember, a child needs to know what is his or hers and have ownership before he or she knows what is ours and is able to share with others.

When a child needs practice with syntax (sequences of words are combined into phrases and sentences) or pragmatics (use of language in social contexts), retelling a favorite story is a great way to assess the sequences of words and phrases.

Art Activity

Help the children make their own colorful footprints. Have an area set up with a shallow pan of tempera paint, a large piece of paper on the floor, a tub of soapy water, and towels. For this activity, you need two adults. One helps the child step into the pan of paint and guides him or her across the paper. The second adult helps the child wash and dry his or her feet.

Supporting Children with Special Needs

If you have a child who is physically unable to make his or her own footprints, paint the child's foot with tempera paint. After his or her foot is painted, blot the foot on a paper towel or a light-colored cloth square. Talk to the child about what is happening. How does it feel? Is it cold? Does it tickle? What color are we using? Are your feet big or small? Let's count your toes, etc.

Simple sign language can enhance instruction and offer another way for the children to prepare to read. For example, when using the poem "Hello" on page 46, fold in your three middle fingers and put your thumb up to your ear and your pinky to your mouth. This is the American Sign Language sign for telephone. Research has shown that typically developing children who have challenges with language will use simple sign language prior to talking.

Enrichment

Cooperative games are fun! To play the game Bees Buzz, have each child find a partner. The teacher says, "Face your partner. Join hands. Say, 'Good afternoon.'" (This sets the mood and makes a connection between the children.) Ask the child to touch body parts with his or her partner. For example, "Put your knees together," or "Touch elbows." After a short time, the teacher says, "Bees buzz." This means it is time for the children to "buzz" around to find a new partner. As soon as all have done this, the game continues.

If one of the children has a baby brother or sister, ask the parent to bring the baby to school. Make a baby puppet for the discussion. A baby puppet can be made out of a baby doll that has a soft body. (Dolls with battery-operated "cry" boxes are available.) Cut a slit in the back of the soft body and remove the stuffing. Place your thumb and pinky finger in the arms and your other fingers in the head. Cradle the head on your other arm and place a receiving blanket over the doll. Move the baby's arms and head slowly. The puppet can be used to begin a conversation with the children about babies and the differences between babies and themselves.

Meeting the Standards: All About Me

Language Arts

- Asks and answers questions
- Comprehends what others are saying
- Demonstrates competency in speaking as a tool for learning
- Demonstrates competency in listening as a tool for learning
- Follows simple directions
- Identifies characters, settings, and important events
- Is developing fine motor skills
- Listens
- Produces rhyming words in response to an oral prompt
- Recites familiar stories and rhymes with patterns
- Recites short stories
- Recognizes meaningful words
- Responds to oral directions
- Responds to oral questions
- Retells familiar stories
- Understands that printed material provides information
- Uses picture clues to aid comprehension
- Uses picture clues to make predictions about content

Mathematics

- Conceptualizes one-to-one correspondence
- Divides objects into categories
- Classifies objects
- Copies and extends patterns
- Explores activities involving chance
- Implements a problem-solving strategy
- Recognizes and collects data
- Uses verbal communication
- Uses pictorial communication
- Uses symbolic communication
- Understands the problem

Science

- Applies problem-solving skills
- Classifies
- Communicates
- Identifies body parts and the five senses
- Identifies objects by color
- Identifies objects by properties
- Identifies objects by shape
- Identifies objects by size
- Predicts
- Problem-solves through group activities
- Recognizes opposites (soft/hard)

Me Poems

I Am Special

I am special, I am special.

(Point to yourself.)

If you look, you will see why,

(Point to the children.)

Someone very special,
someone very special.

It is I! It is I!

(Have the children look in a mirror.)

Friends

(Sing to the tune of "Oh, Do You Know the Muffin Man?")

Oh, will you be a friend of mine,

A friend of mine, a friend of mine?

Oh, will you be a friend of mine,

And love me all the time?

(Stand in front of a child. Hold the child's hands while singing.)

Oh, yes, I'll be a friend of yours,

A friend of yours, a friend of yours,

Oh, yes, I'll be a friend of yours,

(Nod your head.)

And love you all the time.

(Hug the child.)

- -

Teacher Suggestion: Enlarge the poems on this page to display while sharing them.
To promote reading readiness, emphasize the repetitive nature of these poems.

- -

Me Little Me

I went for a sail one very fine day, Yo-Ho, but I was in luck!
(Place the boy and the boat on the upper left hand corner of the flannelboard.)

For as I was sailing my very fine ship, I came upon Chuck the Duck.
(Place the duck on the flannelboard next to the boy.)

There was me little me and Chuck the Duck sailing on a very fine day.
(Point to the boy, the duck, and the sailboat.)

As we were sailing this very fine day, a finer ship no one could wish, we dropped a line into the brine; who joined us but Mish the Fish!
(Place the fish on the flannelboard next to the duck.)

There was me little me, Chuck the Duck, and Mish the Fish sailing on a very fine day.
(Point to the boy, the duck, the fish, and the sailboat.)

As we sailed along this very fine day, steering a steady course, there stood on an isle, grazing a while, a new friend Morse the Horse.
(Place the horse on the flannelboard.)

There was me little me and Chuck the Duck, Mish the Fish, and Morse the Horse, sailing on a very fine day.
(Point to the boy, the duck, the fish, the horse, and the sailboat).

Our sails filled out this very fine day; we came to the Isle of Bermit. There was quite a commotion, when from the dark ocean, we rescued Kermit the Hermit.
(Place the hermit on the flannelboard.)

There was me little me and Chuck the Duck, Mish the Fish, Morse the Horse, and Kermit the Hermit sailing on a very fine day.
(Point to the boy, the duck, the fish, the horse, the hermit, and the sailboat.)

As we were sailing this very fine day, the wind got very tricky. Afloat with no boat, but a buoy 'round his throat, we discovered Mickey the Chickey.
(Place the chicken on the flannelboard.)

There was me little me and Chuck the Duck, Mish the Fish, Morse the Horse, Kermit the Hermit, and Mickey the Chickey sailing on a very fine day.
(Point to the boy, the duck, the fish, the horse, the hermit, the chicken, and the sailboat.)

We went so fast this very fine day; Yo-Ho our dinghy broke loose. Oh my, we were lucky, for a friend so plucky, brought it back—'twas Bruce the Goose.
(Place the goose on the flannelboard.)

Me Little Me *(cont.)*

There was me little me and Chuck the Duck, Mish the Fish, Morse the Horse, Kermit the Hermit, Mickey the Chickey, and Bruce the Goose sailing on a very fine day.

(Point to the boy, the duck, the fish, the horse, the hermit, the chicken, the goose, and the sailboat.)

As we were sailing this very fine day, the sea looked blue and pretty. With glass to my eye, whom did I spy, but my old friend Smitty the Kitty?

(Place the kitty on the flannelboard.)

There was me little me and Chuck the Duck, Mish the Fish, Morse the Horse, Kermit the Hermit, Mickey the Chickey, Bruce the Goose, and Smitty the Kitty sailing on a very fine day.

(Point to the boy, the duck, the fish, the horse, the hermit, the chicken, the goose, the kitty, and the sailboat.)

The wind went down, our fine ship tossed, 'twas night, very late, 8 o'clock. When there came unafraid Muriel the Mermaid, who towed us back to the dock.

(Place the mermaid on the flannelboard.)

There was me little me and Chuck the Duck, Mish the Fish, Morse the Horse, Kermit the Hermit, Mickey the Chickey, Bruce the Goose, Smitty the Kitty, and Muriel the Mermaid sailing on a very fine day.

(Point to the boy, the duck, the fish, the horse, the hermit, the chicken, the goose, the kitty, the mermaid, and the sailboat.)

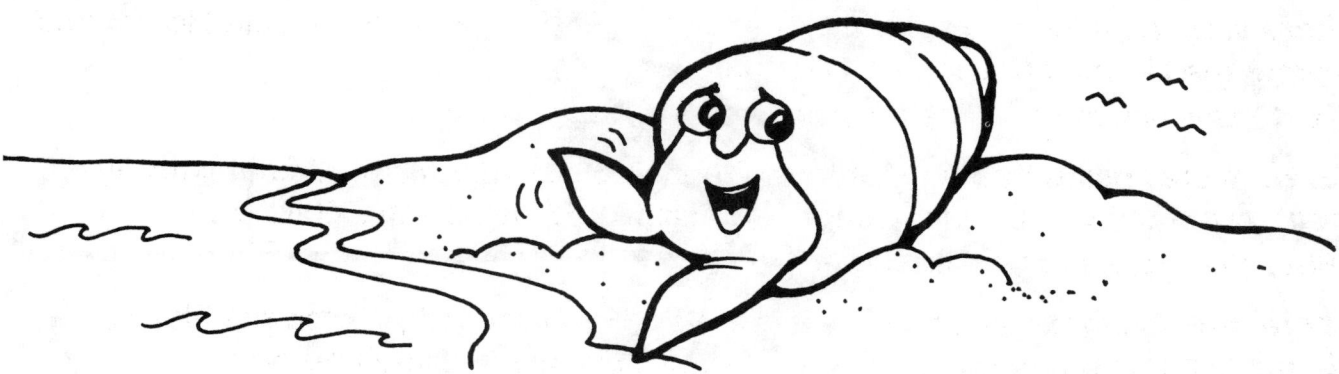

Use the pattern on page 22 to create the boy. Use the patterns above and on pages 36-38 to create the sailboat, Chuck the Duck, Mish the Fish, Morse the Horse, Kermit the Hermit, Mickey the Chickey, Bruce the Goose, Smitty the Kitty, and Muriel the Mermaid flannel pieces.

Patterns for Me Little Me

Kermit the Hermit

Morse the Horse

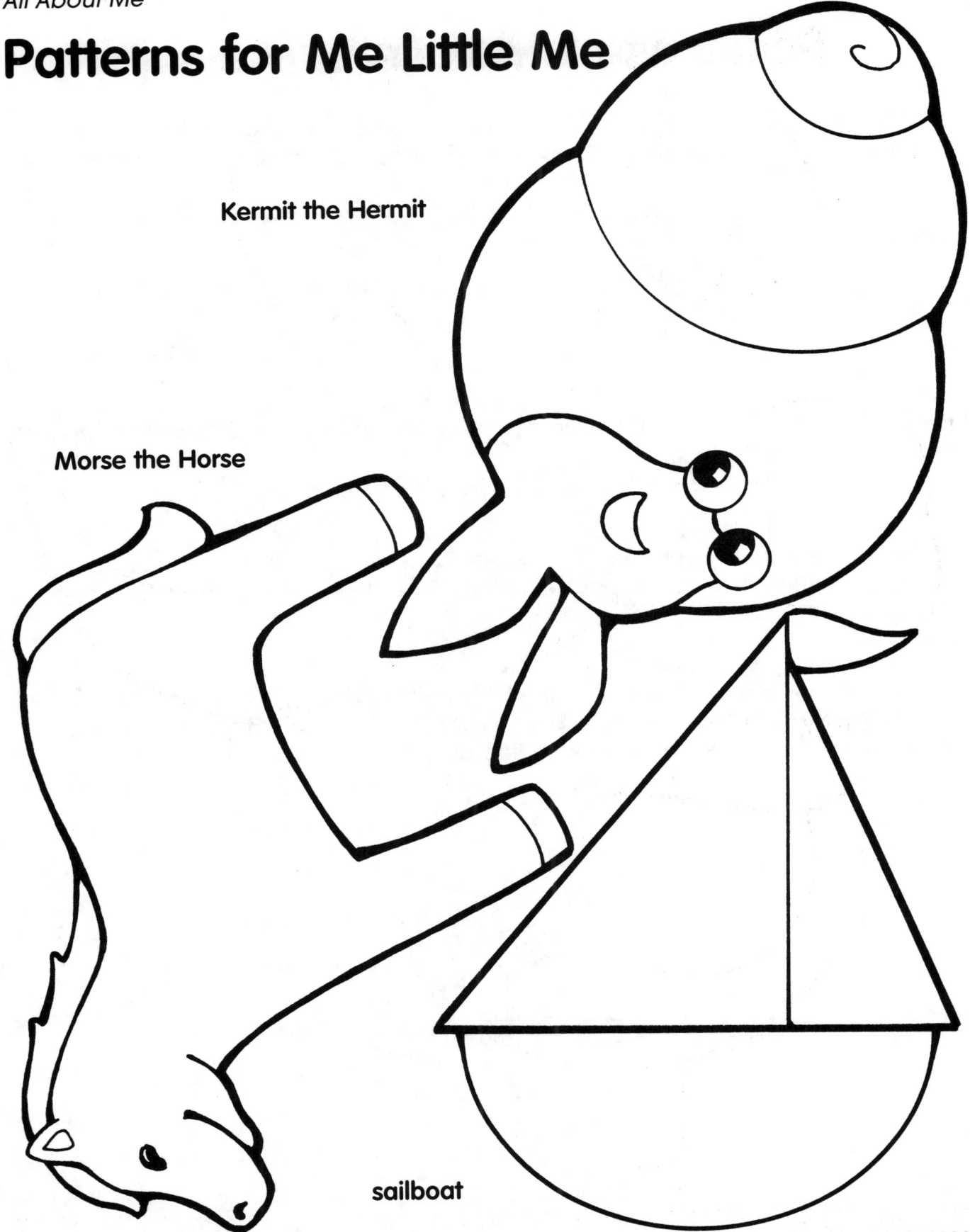

sailboat

1. Make one sailboat. 2. Make one Morse the Horse. 3. Make one Kermit the Hermit.

36

Patterns for Me Little Me *(cont.)*

Bruce the Goose

Smitty the Kitty

Chuck the Duck

1. Make one Chuck the Duck.
2. Make one Bruce the Goose.

3. Make one Smitty the Kitty.

Patterns for Me Little Me *(cont.)*

Mish the Fish

Mickey the Chickey

Muriel the Mermaid

1. Make one Mish the Fish.
2. Make one Mickey the Chickey.
3. Make one Muriel the Mermaid.

Ball for Baby

Here's a ball for baby, big and soft and round.
(Put the baby and the ball on the flannelboard.)

Here's baby's hammer, pound-a, pound-a, pound!
(Place the hammer on the flannelboard.)

Here is baby's music, clapping, clapping, so!
(Put the musical notes on the flannelboard and clap your hands.)

Here are baby's soldiers, standing in a row.
(Place the row of soldiers on the flannelboard.)

Here's the baby's trumpet, toot-too-toot! too-too!
(Put the trumpet on the flannelboard.)

Here's the way that baby plays at "peek-a-boo."
(Cover your eyes with your fingers. Bring your fingers to the sides of your face so your eyes are visible. Say, "Peek-a-boo.")

Here's a big umbrella. Keep the baby dry.
(Place the umbrella on the flannelboard.)

Here's the baby's cradle, rock-a-baby-bye!
(Put the baby in the cradle on the flannelboard.)

• •

Use the patterns on pages 40-42 to create the baby, the ball, the hammer, the musical notes, the row of soldiers, the trumpet, the umbrella, and the baby-in-a-cradle flannel pieces.

• •

Patterns for Ball for Baby

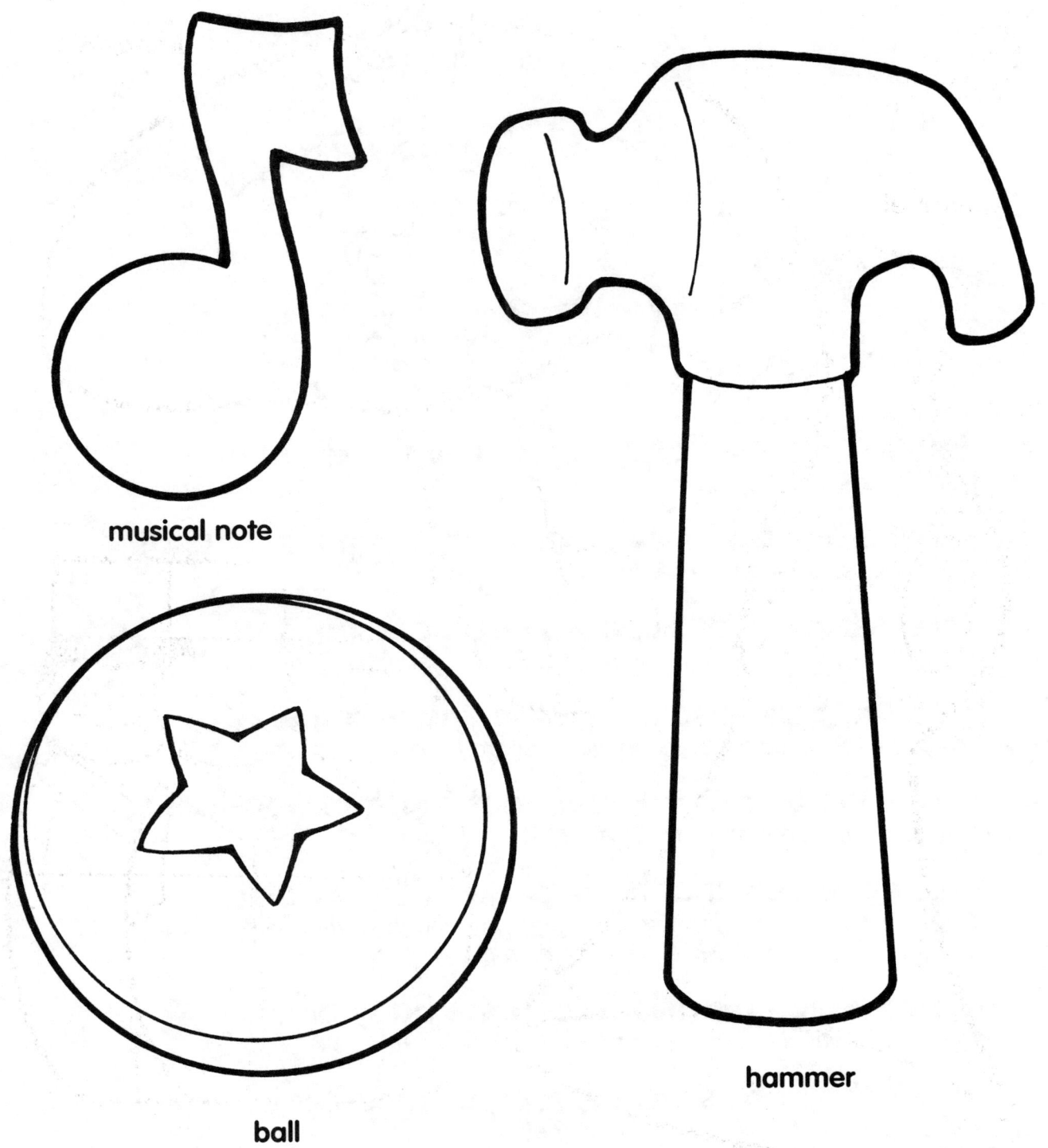

musical note

ball

hammer

1. Make one ball.
2. Make one hammer.
3. Make several musical notes.

40

Patterns for Ball for Baby *(cont.)*

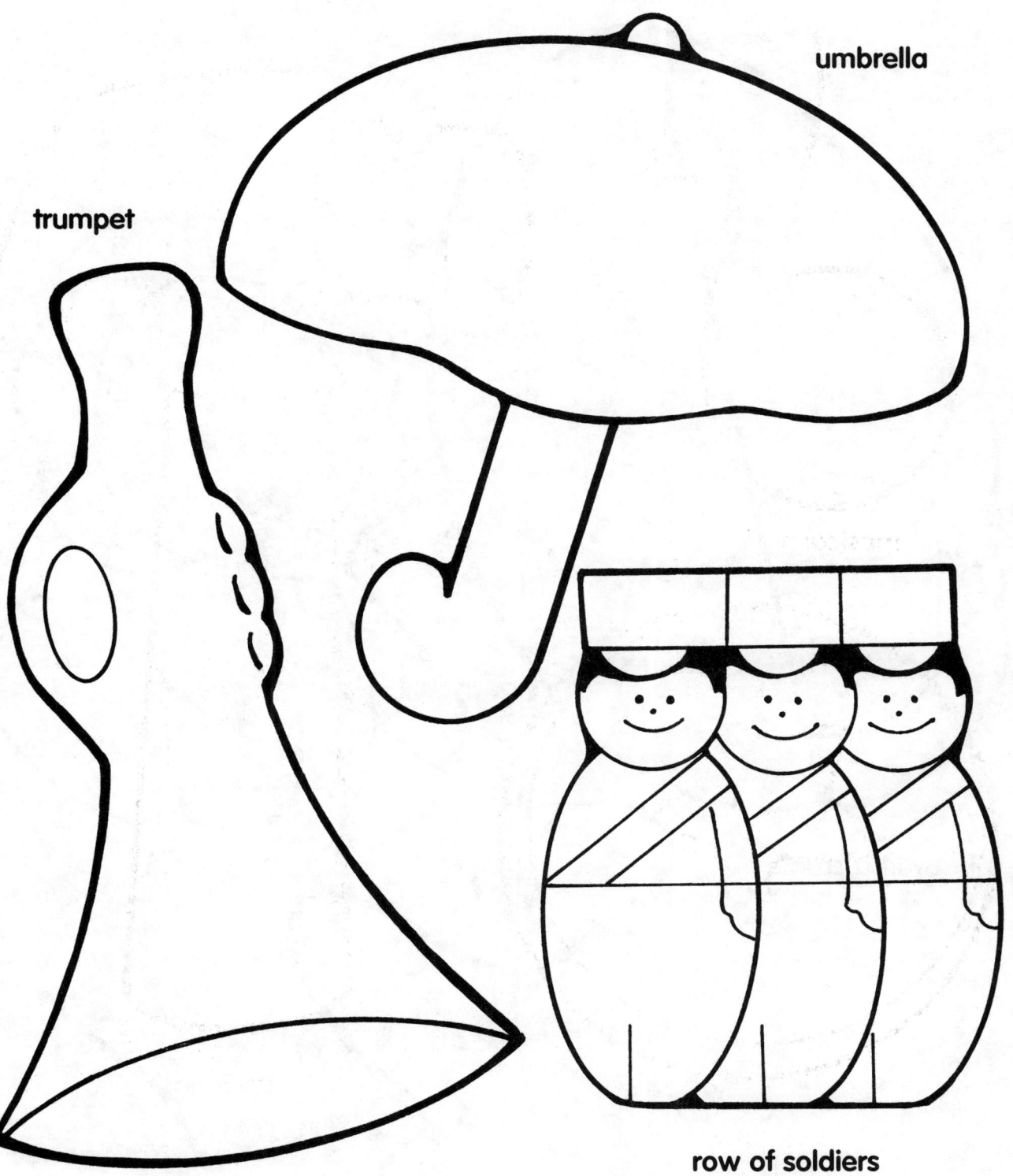

umbrella

trumpet

row of soldiers

. . . .

1. Make one row of soldiers.
2. Make one trumpet.
3. Make one umbrella.

. . . .

Patterns for Ball for Baby *(cont.)*

baby in a cradle

sitting baby

∙∙

1. Make one baby in a cradle.
2. Make one sitting baby.

∙∙

Body Poems

I Wiggle My Fingers

I wiggle my fingers.
(Hold your hands up in front of your chest and wiggle your fingers.)

I wiggle my toes.
(Extend your feet and pretend to wiggle your toes.)

I wiggle my shoulders.
(Move your shoulders forward and back.)

I wiggle my nose.
(Place your index finger on your nose and wiggle it.)

No more wiggles are left in me.

So I will sit down, as still as can be.
(Sit down and be very still.)

The Touch Game

Touch your nose.
(Put your hands on your nose.)

Touch your chin.
(Move your hands down to your chin.)

That's the way this game begins.

Touch your eyes.
(Gently cover your eyes.)

Touch your knees.
(Put one hand on each knee.)

Now pretend you are going to sneeze.
(Bring your wrist up under your nose.)

Touch your hair.
(Put both of your hands on your hair.)

Touch one ear.
(Place one hand on an ear.)

Touch your two red lips right here.
(Take the fingertips of your hands up to your lips—let go as if blowing a kiss.)

Touch your elbows where they bend.
(Use one hand to touch one elbow.)

That's the way this touch game ends.

• •

Teacher Suggestion: After you say each line, pause to wait for the children to make the hand motion indicated in the rhyme.

• •

Here I Am

This is the circle that is my head.
(Place the circle on the flannelboard.)

This is my mouth where words are said.
(Place the serious mouth on the head.)

Here are my eyes, with which I see.
(Place two eyes on the head.)

And here's my nose that's a part of me.
(Place the nose on the head.)

This is the hair that grows on my head.
(Place the hair on the head.)

And here's a hat, so bright and red.
(Place the red hat on the head.)

My smile will show you I'm happy today.
(Replace the serious mouth with the smiling mouth on the head.)

And glad to go to school and play.

• •

Use the patterns on page 45 to make the pieces for this flannelboard story or to create stick puppets.

Teacher Suggestion: After the story has been told once, have a variety of materials available for the children to create faces that represent themselves. Have the children recite the poem using their own flannel pieces or stick puppets.

• •

Patterns for Here I Am

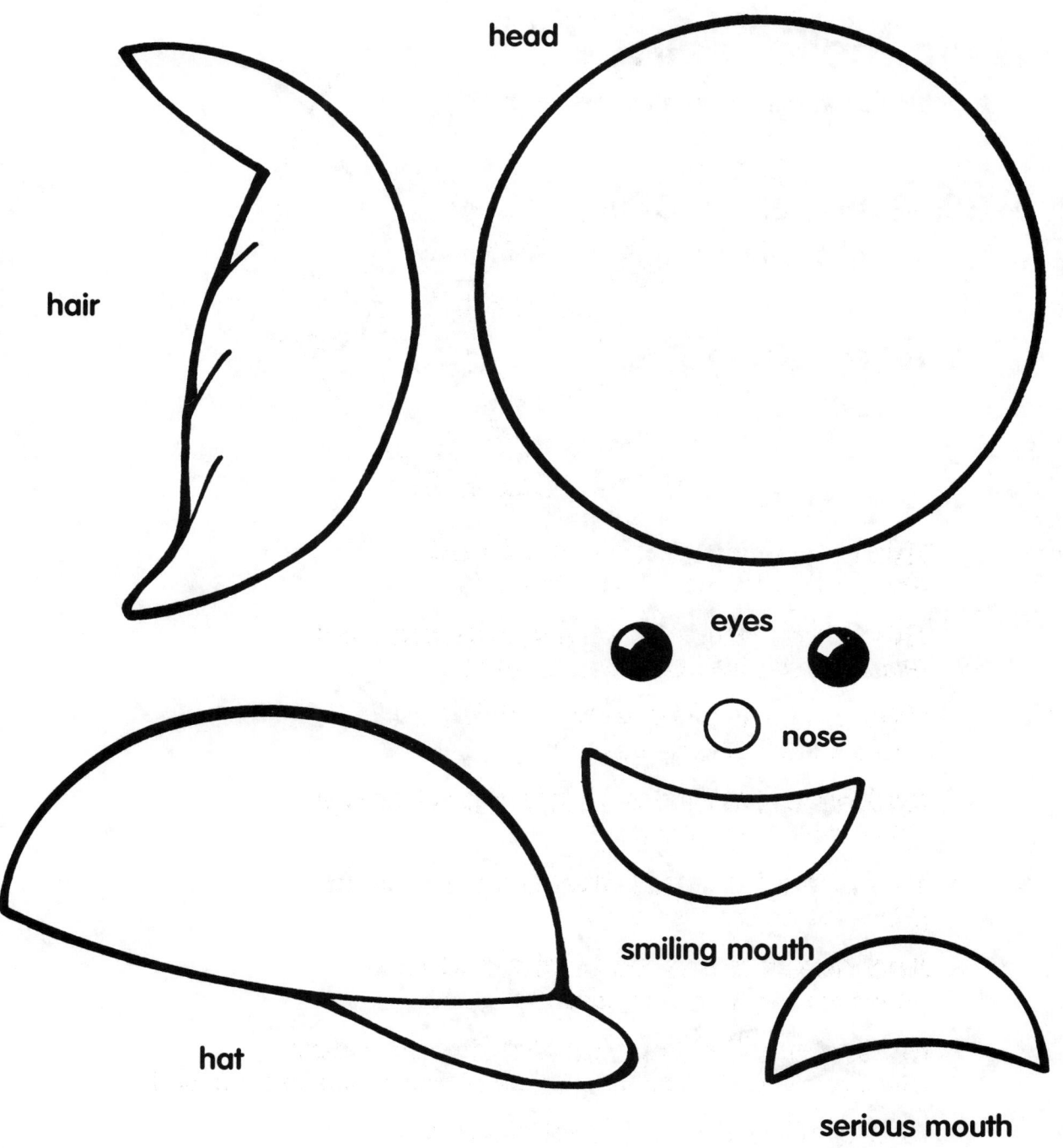

head

hair

eyes

nose

smiling mouth

hat

serious mouth

1. Make one large circle for the head.
2. Make one serious mouth.
3. Make one smiling mouth.
4. Make two eyes.
5. Make one nose.
6. Make one red hat.
7. Make some hair.

Hello

Hello, hello, hello.
(Hold the cardboard telephone up to your ear.)

And how are you?
(Point to one of the children.)

I'm fine, I'm fine.
(Point to yourself.)

And I hope

That you are too.
(Point to one of the children.)

telephone

Have each child make a cardboard telephone, using the pattern above. If needed, enlarge the telephone pattern and copy it onto cardstock.

Teacher Suggestion: Use the American Sign Language sign for telephone in place of a cardboard telephone. To make the sign, place your thumb by your ear and your pinky by your mouth.

My Hands

These are my hands.

This is my right hand; I'll raise it high.
(Raise your right hand above your head.)

This my left hand; I'll touch the sky.
(Raise your left hand above your head.)

Right hand.   *(Shake your right hand.)*
Left hand.   *(Shake your left hand.)*

Roll them around.
(Roll your hands around in front of your stomach.)

Left hand.   *(Shake your left hand.)*
Right hand.   *(Shake your right hand.)*

These are my hands.
(Hold up both of your hands in the air.)

Clap, clap, clap, they fall into my lap.
(Clap and put your hands in your lap.)

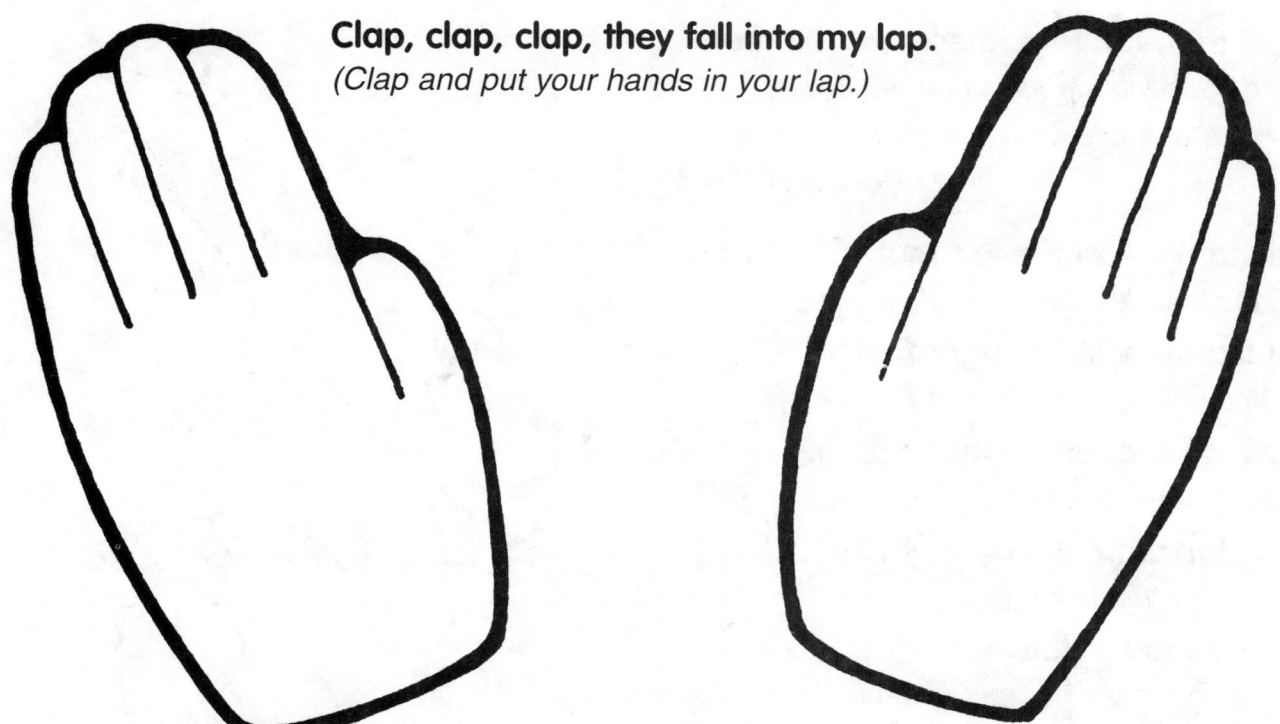

Use the patterns above to create the left and right hand stick puppets.
1. Make and color one right hand stick puppet.
2. Make one left hand stick puppet using a different color.

Left and Right Poems

My Feet

These are my feet.
This is my right foot, tap, tap, tap.
(Extend your right foot and tap it on the ground.)

This is my left foot, pat, pat, pat.
(Reach down and pat your left foot.)

Right foot, left foot.
(Hold each foot up as you name it.)

Run, run, run.
(Run in place.)

Left foot, right foot.
(Hold each foot up as you name it.)

Jump, jump for fun.
(Jump up and down in place.)

Right foot, left foot, these are my feet.
(Hold each foot up as you name it.)

We Know Left and Right

We stamp with the left foot.
(Stamp your left foot down firmly.)

We stamp with the right foot.
(Stamp your right foot down firmly.)

Then we turn ourselves around.
(Turn all the way around.)

And clap with all our might.
(Clap your hands loudly.)

We look to the left side.
(Move your head sharply to the left side of your body.)

Then look to the right side.
(Move your head sharply to the right side of your body.)

We step forward.
(Take a step forward.)

We step backward.
(Take a step backward.)

Mouse Unit

Young children are fascinated by mouse stories. Use this high interest and motivation to enhance your reading readiness program. Each story in this unit has a message to learn. For example, Timothy Mouse learns to listen. The stories can be told and then used to reinforce important skills during classroom activity time.

Teaching Tips

One of the primary reasons we use finger plays, puppets, and flannelboard stories is to introduce materials to children prior to the actual teaching of a concept. This exposure is done often enough for young children to actually learn the concept. Sometimes the activity serves as a mnemonic for remembering the concept later during the instructional lesson (for example, "Let's all be good listeners like Timothy Mouse.")

Art Activity

Give each child a small amount of clay. Have him or her manipulate the clay to form a mouse. Show the children how to roll the balls and put them together to form a mouse. When the child has finished using the clay, have him or her roll it in a ball and insert his or her thumb into the ball. Fill the cavity that the thumb made in the ball with water. This keeps the clay moist and pliable and ready to use the next day. (Clay has different texture than play dough and can be used over and over. If desired, allow the children's mouse sculptures to dry out.)

Supporting Children with Special Needs

Play therapists have researched puppet play and found that many times children will talk to a puppet and say things to it that they otherwise would not share with you. Show to the children a mouse puppet that acts shy and talks to you about being shy. Ask the children if they would like to speak to the puppet. When a child is very shy or is lacking verbal language skills, encourage the child to "talk" to the mouse puppet.

Enrichment

Play the game "Cat and Mouse." Make a large circle with all of the children holding hands. The child in the center is the mouse and the child outside of the circle is the cat. The cat tries to run under the ring of arms to get into the house to catch the mouse. If the cat enters the circle, the mouse runs out. This is a great game to introduce the poem, "Great Big Cat and Teeny Little Mouse." Before reading the book *Mouse Paint,* by Ed Young, make a batch of Rainbow Stew. In addition to being a great science experience, this activity enhances small muscle coordination. Children who are stressed often find this activity calming.

Rainbow Stew

1 cup cornstarch	4 cups water
1/3 cup sugar	food coloring (yellow, red, and blue)

1. Mix the cornstarch, sugar, and water together and cook until thick.
2. Divide the batter into three bowls. Add red food coloring to one, yellow to the second, and blue to the third.
3. Set the bowls on the table. Direct each child to choose two colors. Have him or her place one spoonful of each into a resealable, plastic bag.
4. Seal the bag. Let the children squeeze their bags until the two colors create a new color.

Meeting the Standards: Mouse Unit

Language Arts

- Asks and answers questions
- Comprehends what others are saying
- Demonstrates competency in speaking as a tool for learning
- Demonstrates competency in listening as a tool for learning
- Follows simple directions
- Identifies and sorts common shape words into basic categories
- Identifies characters, settings, and important events
- Is developing fine motor skills
- Listens
- Recites short stories
- Recognizes meaningful words
- Responds to oral directions
- Responds to oral questions
- Uses picture clues to aid comprehension
- Uses picture clues to make predictions about content

Mathematics

- Divides objects into categories
- Estimates quantities
- Explores activities involving chance
- Identifies equal/unequal portions
- Identifies shapes in different positions
- Identifies shapes in the real world
- Implements a problem-solving strategy
- Makes predictions
- Recognizes and collects data
- Solves simple equations
- Uses pictorial communication
- Uses symbolic communication
- Uses verbal communication

Science

- Applies problem-solving skills
- Explores animals
- Identifies color in the real world
- Identifies objects by properties
- Identifies objects by shape
- Identifies object by size
- Observes, identifies, and measures objects
- Problem-solves through group activities

Five Little Mice

(Place the tree, the picnic basket, the sun, and the blanket on the flannelboard.)

Five little mice were happy as could be,
Having a picnic beneath a great tree.
(Place the family of mice at the picnic scene.)

Papa Mouse rose and went to the shore,
Far away he walked, and then there were four.
(Show Papa Mouse walking across the flannelboard and off.)

Mama Mouse nibbled and then went to see
Where he had gone, and then there were three.
(Remove Mama Mouse from the scene.)

Big Brother Mouse couldn't find his new shoe,
He went to look for it and then there were two.
(Remove Big Brother Mouse from the scene.)

Little Brother Mouse wanted
to play and have fun.

He ran, and he hid, and then
there was one.
(Show Little Brother scurrying across the flannelboard and off.)

Little Sister Mouse, alone in
the sun,

Searched for her brother.
(Show Little Sister Mouse looking around and then remove her from the scene.)

Then there were none!

Use the patterns on pages 52–55 to create the tree, the mouse family, the sun, and the picnic basket.

Patterns for Five Little Mice *(cont.)*

....

1. Enlarge the tree and color it.

....

Patterns for Five Little Mice

Mama Mouse

Papa Mouse

1. Make one Papa Mouse.
2. Make one Mama Mouse.

Mouse

Patterns for Five Little Mice *(cont.)*

Big Brother Mouse

Little Sister Mouse

Little Brother Mouse

....

1. Make one Big Brother Mouse.
2. Make one Little Brother Mouse.
3. Make one Little Sister Mouse.

....

Patterns for Five Little Mice *(cont.)*

sun

picnic basket

1. Make one sun.
2. Make one picnic basket.
3. Make one colorful picnic blanket using different colored felt.

My Friend the Mouse

By Kim Fields

My friend the mouse
Is as quick as can be,
(Move the mouse back and forth in front of you.)

He hurries and scurries
And likes to chase me.
(Spin around in a circle holding the mouse.)

My friend the mouse
Is as clever as can be,
(Tap the mouse's head to your head.)

He's squeaky and sneaky
And likes to hide from me.
(Move the mouse behind your back.)

My friend the mouse
Is as cute as can be,
(Dance the mouse in front of you.)

He's sweet and petite
And likes to hug me.
(Hug the mouse.)

Create a mouse stick puppet using the large mouse pattern above.

As Small As a Mouse

Make yourself tall.
(Hold your hands above your head.)

Make yourself small.
(Squat down, place your hands near the floor.)

Make yourself flat.
(Hold your hands together, fingers straight.)

Make yourself fat.
(Hold your arms out in a rounded shape.)

Make yourself as big as a house.
(Stretch your hands out.)

Make yourself as small as a mouse.
*(Squat with your head down,
holding your legs with your hands to form a ball shape.)*

Timothy Mouse

Once upon a time there was a little mouse named Timothy. Timothy always wore a hat.

(Put Timothy Mouse with his hat on the flannelboard, making certain the hat covers his ears!)

He wore a hat because he didn't have any ears, and he didn't have any ears because he wouldn't LISTEN. So he wore his hat all day and all night. And he never took it off! Timothy never listened to anyone. He did whatever he wanted to. He did not listen to his mother. He did not listen to his father. He did not listen to his teachers, and he did not listen to his friends.

(Sadly shake your head back and forth.)

One day when Timothy was walking along he met Betty Bunny.

(Place Betty Bunny on the flannelboard.)

"Oh," said Timothy, "what are those beautiful things you have on your head?"

(Point to Betty Bunny's ears.)

"Those are my ears," said Betty Bunny.

"Where did you get those beautiful ears?"

"Why, I've always had them. I got them by listening, of course," said Betty Bunny. "I always listen to everybody. I listen to my mother. I listen to my father. I listen to my teachers and I listen to my friends. If you just listen, your ears will grow bigger and bigger. That's all there is to it."

So Timothy thought about that. "I think I'll try it," he said. And he did. That very day he began to listen to things. He listened when his mother talked to him. He listened when his father talked to him. He listened to his teachers and his friends. He found he had a lot more fun when he listened.

(Shake your head up and down.)

One day Timothy thought his hat felt funny on his head. He felt his head.

(Feel your head with your hand.)

There were lumps under his hat. He went to the mirror. Took off his hat. And there under his hat were the best pair of mouse ears you have ever seen.

(Remove the hat from Timothy's head.)

• •

Use the patterns on page 59 to create the Timothy Mouse, Betty Bunny, and stocking hat flannel pieces.

Teacher Suggestion: This story can be told using hand puppets. Refer to the directions on page 14 to create puppets from bunny and mouse stuffed animals. Use a stocking hat for Timothy Mouse's hat.

Patterns for Timothy Mouse

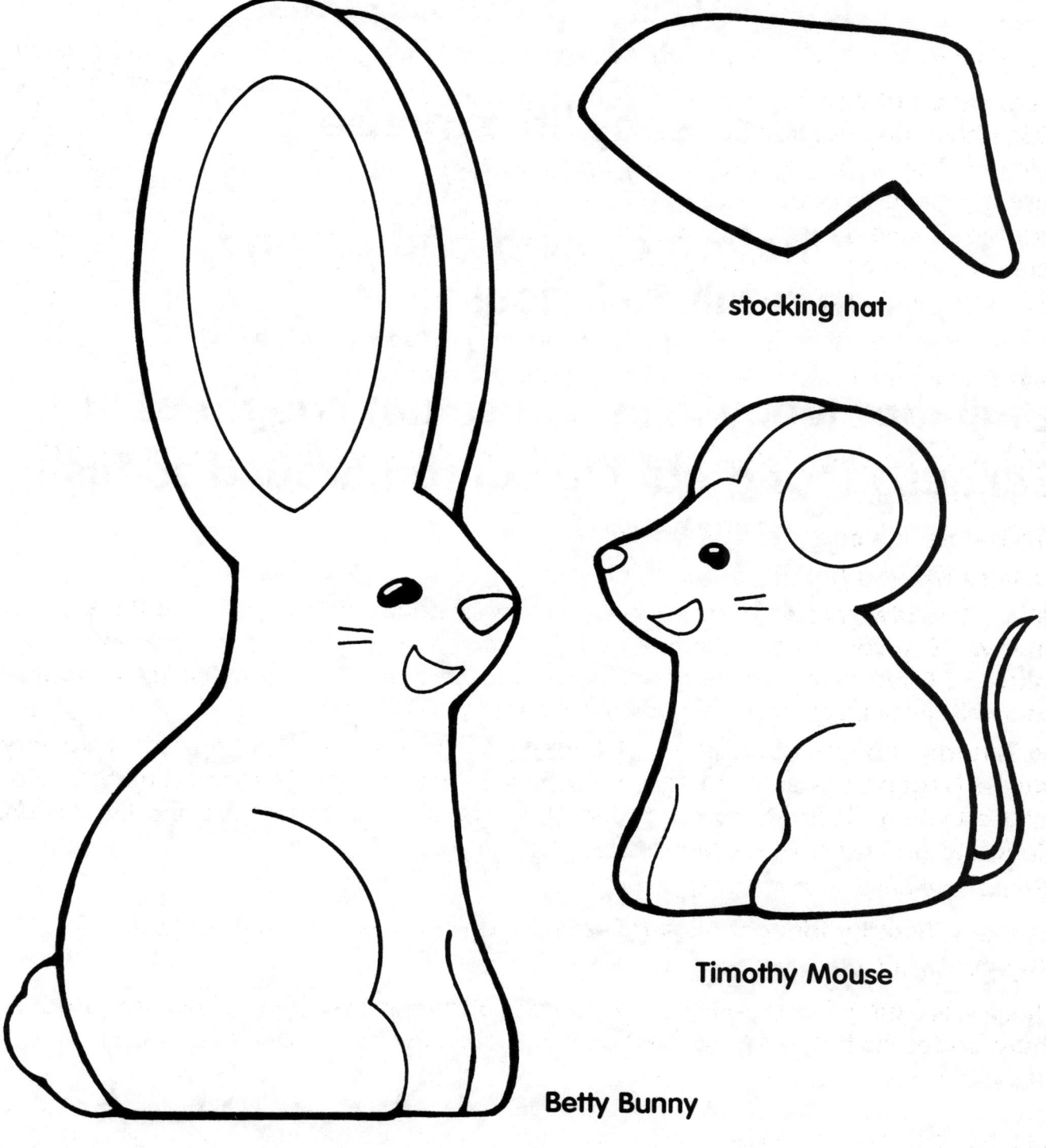

stocking hat

Timothy Mouse

Betty Bunny

1. Make one stocking hat.
2. Make one Timothy Mouse.
3. Make one Betty Bunny.

Great Big Cat and Teeny Little Mouse

There was a great big cat
(Put the cat on the flannelboard.)

And a teeny little mouse
(Put the mouse on the flannelboard.)

Who ran around and around
in a tall, tall, house!
(Move the cat and mouse around the flannelboard house.)

Until that teeny little mouse got caught at last.
Because that great big cat ran around so fast!
(Move the cat until he catches the mouse.)

Use the patterns on page 61 to create the great big cat, teeny little mouse, and house flannel pieces.

Patterns for Great Big Cat and Teeny Little Mouse

house

great big cat

teeny little mouse

1. Make one great big cat.
2. Make one teeny little mouse. Add a piece of yarn for a tail.
3. Make one house.

Dinosaur Unit

Young children are fascinated with dinosaurs. Children may even memorize the names of dinosaurs before they know the names of their classmates. Use this motivation and fascination with dinosaurs to enhance your reading readiness curriculum.

Teaching Tips

Enlarge the dinosaur patterns in this unit and create a classroom mural. Have the children participate in sponge painting the dinosaurs for the mural and then label each dinosaur with its name and some key facts. When you need a filler activity, read the names and review the selected material.

Reinforce the concepts learned during the dinosaur unit by creating a paper-plate game for small-group time. To make the game, use a brad to secure a cardboard arrow (for the spinner) to the center of a paper plate. Divide the plate into sections and attach a dinosaur sticker or pattern (provided in this unit) to each section. To play the game, a child spins the arrow. Then, he or she chooses a rhyme or fact to share about that dinosaur.

Art Activities

Make dinosaur skeletons. Draw an outline of a dinosaur with white chalk on a sheet of dark, heavy paper. Cut paper or newspaper into strips and twist them into long rows to make the dinosaur's bones. Glue the "bones" on the dark paper in the appropriate places.

Make a dinosaur diorama. Use a large cardboard box filled partly with sand or the sandbox to create the dinosaur diorama. Add miniature plastic dinosaurs, plastic bones, small rocks, pebbles, leaves, and moss. Ask students to use the items to depict scenes from the dinosaur poems and stories in this unit.

Supporting Children with Special Needs

Children with special needs need non-threatening opportunities to participate in activities. For example, when presenting the poem, "One Dinosaur Went Out to Play" (page 64), walk around the room imitating a dinosaur. Then, motion for another "dinosaur" child to come and join you. Hold hands with the child and repeat the actions. Once several children have joined you, link your hands with the child with special needs. The child will follow the simple model provided by you and the other children and will enjoy the role play.

Enrichment

As you are transitioning from one activity to another, have the children pretend they are dinosaurs. For example, have them move like an Apatosaurus (slowly) or a Compsognathus (quickly), fly like a Pteranodon, or eat like an Allosaurus.

Meeting the Standards: Dinosaur Unit

Language Arts

- Asks and answers questions
- Demonstrates competency in speaking as a tool for learning
- Demonstrates competency in listening as a tool for learning
- Identifies and sorts common shape words into basic categories
- Identifies characters, settings, and important events
- Listens
- Produces meaningful linguistic sounds
- Produces rhyming words in response to an oral prompt
- Recites familiar stories and rhymes with patterns
- Recites short stories
- Recognizes meaningful words
- Responds to oral directions
- Retells familiar stories

Mathematics

- Classifies objects
- Conceptualizes one-to-one correspondences
- Divides objects into categories
- Makes predictions
- Recognizes and collects data
- Uses verbal communication
- Uses pictorial communication
- Uses symbolic communication
- Understands the problem

Science

- Applies problem-solving skills
- Discusses changes in seasons
- Explores reptiles
- Explores animals
- Identifies objects by properties
- Identifies objects by size
- Observes, identifies, and measures objects
- Problem-solves through group activities

Dinosaur

One Dinosaur Went Out to Play

(Sing to the tune of "One Elephant Went Out to Play.")

One Triceratops went out to play.
(Put Triceratops on the flannelboard.)

Out in the world of yesterday.
He had such enormous fun.
He called for his friend Tyrannosaurus Rex to come.
(Place Tyrannosaurus Rex on the flannelboard.)

One Tyrannosaurus Rex went out to play.
Out in the world of yesterday.
He had such enormous fun.
He called for his friend Stegosaurus to come.
(Put Stegosaurus on the flannelboard.)

One Stegosaurus went out to play.
Out in the world of yesterday.
He had such enormous fun.
He called for his friend Trachodon to come.
(Put Trachodon on the flannelboard.)

One Trachodon went out to play.
Out in the world of yesterday.
He had such enormous fun.
He called for his friend Dimetrodon to come.
(Place Dimetrodon on the flannelboard.)

One Dimetrodon went out to play.
Out in the world of yesterday.
He had such enormous fun.
He called for his friend Apatosaurus to come.
(Place Apatosaurus on the flannelboard.)

One Apatosaurus went out to play.
Out in the world of yesterday.
He had such enormous fun.
He stayed and played till the day was done.

Enlarge the patterns on pages 65-67 to create Triceratops, Tyrannosaurus Rex, Stegosaurus, Trachodon, Dimetrodon, and Apatosaurus stick puppets.

Patterns for One Dinosaur
Went Out to Play

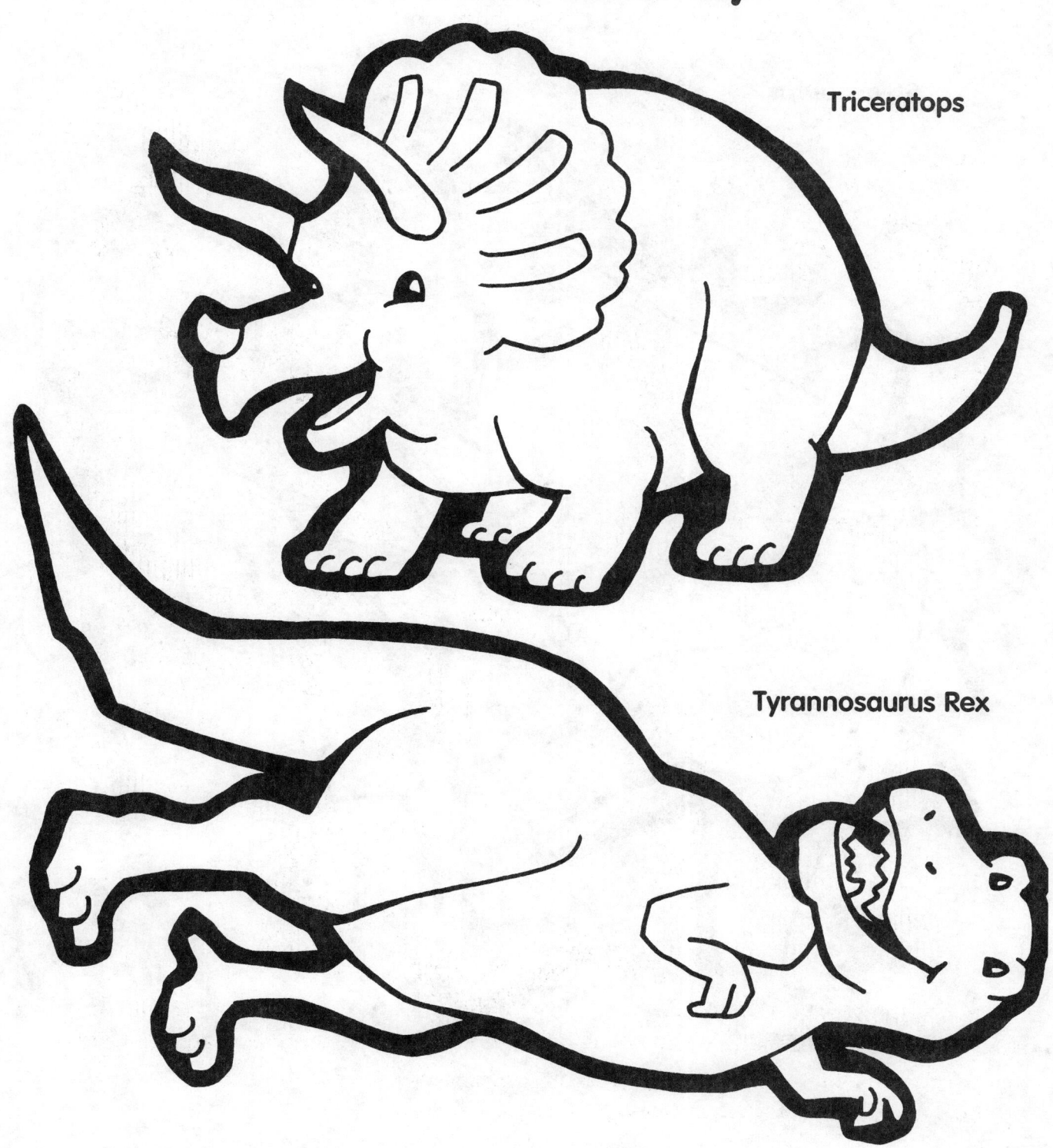

Triceratops

Tyrannosaurus Rex

· ·

1. Make one Triceratops.   2. Make one Tyrannosaurus Rex.

· ·

Patterns for One Dinosaur
Went Out to Play *(cont.)*

Stegosaurus

Trachodon

. . . .
1. Make one Stegosaurus.   2. Make one Trachodon.
. . . .

Patterns for One Dinosaur
Went Out to Play *(cont.)*

Dimetrodon

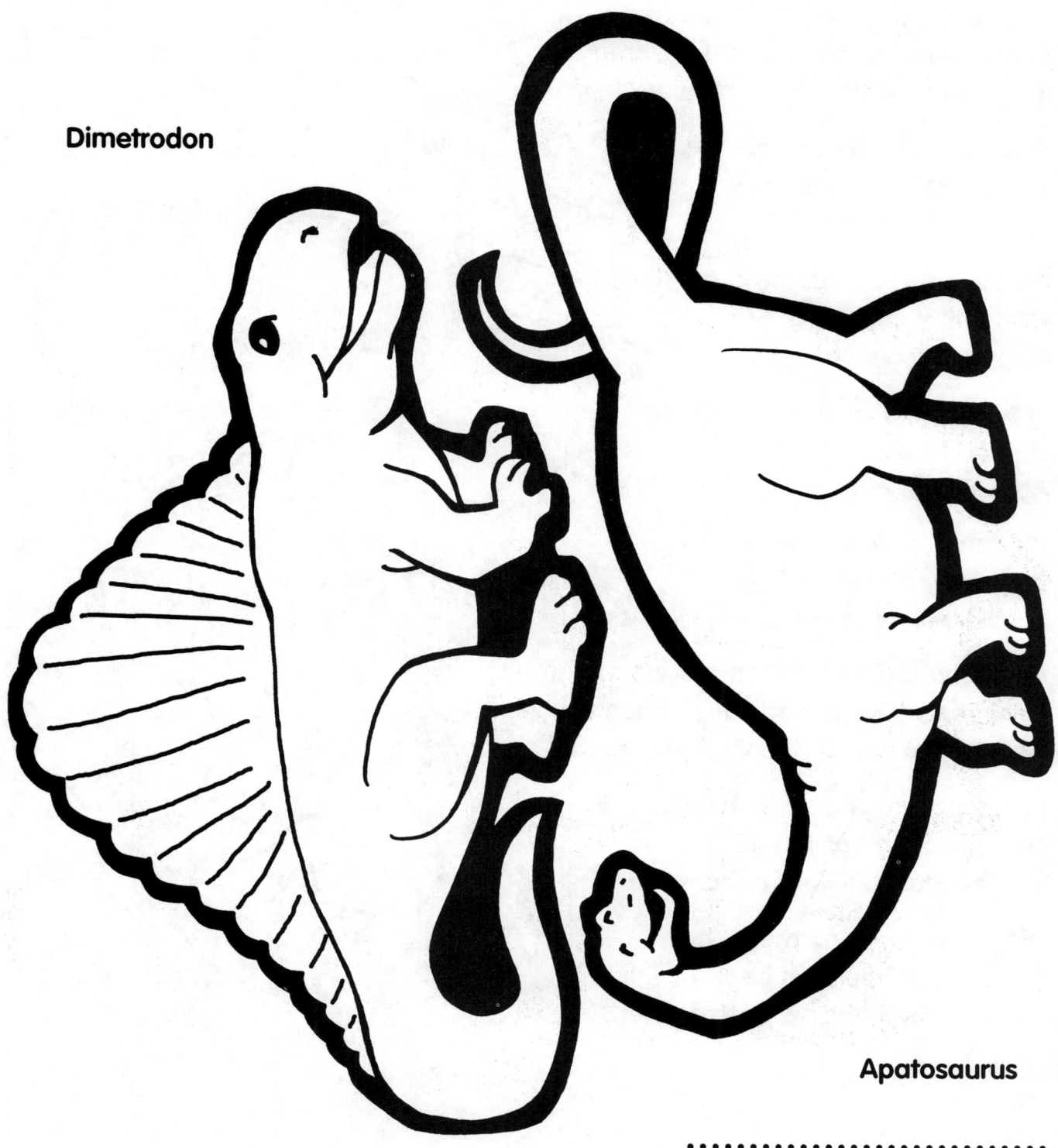

Apatosaurus

....

1. Make one Dimetrodon.
2. Make one Apatosaurus.

....

Dinosaur History

Dinosaurs lived long ago.
They walked the earth to and fro.
Some were big and some were small.
Some were short and some were tall.

Stegosaurus was big, not tall.
The plates down his back
protected him from all.

Allosaurus was scary to see.
His teeth were sharp,
He really scares me.

Triceratops was short and stout.
He had three horns
Above his snout.

Pteranodon had leathery wings.
So he could soar and glide.
Someone told me he could even sing!

Apatosaurus liked to stomp upon the ground.
He was very large and could reach very high.
He loved to munch the trees all around.

Tyrannosaurus Rex, boy he was tall.
This dinosaur was the fiercest one.
Yes, he was the king of them all.

Dinosaurs roam no more.
They can be found in books, I think,
Because the dinosaurs are extinct.

. . . .

Use the patterns on pages 65-67 and 69 to create the Allosaurus, Pteranodon, Triceratops, Tyrannosaurus Rex, Stegosaurus, and Apatosaurus stick puppets.

. . . .

Patterns for Dinosaur History

Allosaurus

Pteranodon

1. Make one Allosaurus.
2. Make one Pteranodon.
3. Make one Triceratops and one Tyrannosaurus Rex using the patterns on page 65.
4. Make one Stegosaurus using the pattern on page 66.
5. Make one Apatosaurus using the pattern on page 67.

Dinosaurs, Where Are You?

(Sing to the tune of "Are You Sleeping?")

Brachiosaurus, Brachiosaurus,
Where are you? Where are you?
Your head is in the water; your head is in the water.
Your tail is, too! Your tail is, too!

Stegosaurus, Stegosaurus,
Where are you? Where are you?
Your back has sharp points;
your back has sharp points.
Your tail does, too! Your tail does, too!

Apatosaurus, Apatosaurus,
Where are you? Where are you?
Your neck is so long; your neck is so long.
Your tail is, too! Your tail is, too!

Tyrannosaurus Rex, Tyrannosaurus Rex,
Where are you? Where are you?
Your jaws are so big;
your jaws are so big.
Your teeth are, too!
Your teeth are, too!

Use the patterns on pages 65–67 and 71 to create the Brachiosaurus, Tyrannosaurus Rex, Stegosaurus, and Apatosaurus stick puppets. Use a piece of blue cloth for the water.

Pattern for
Dinosaurs, Where Are You?

• •

1. Make one Brachiosaurus.
2. Make one Tyrannosaurus Rex using the pattern on page 65.
3. Make one Stegosaurus using the pattern on page 66.
4. Make one Apatosaurus using the pattern on page 67.

• •

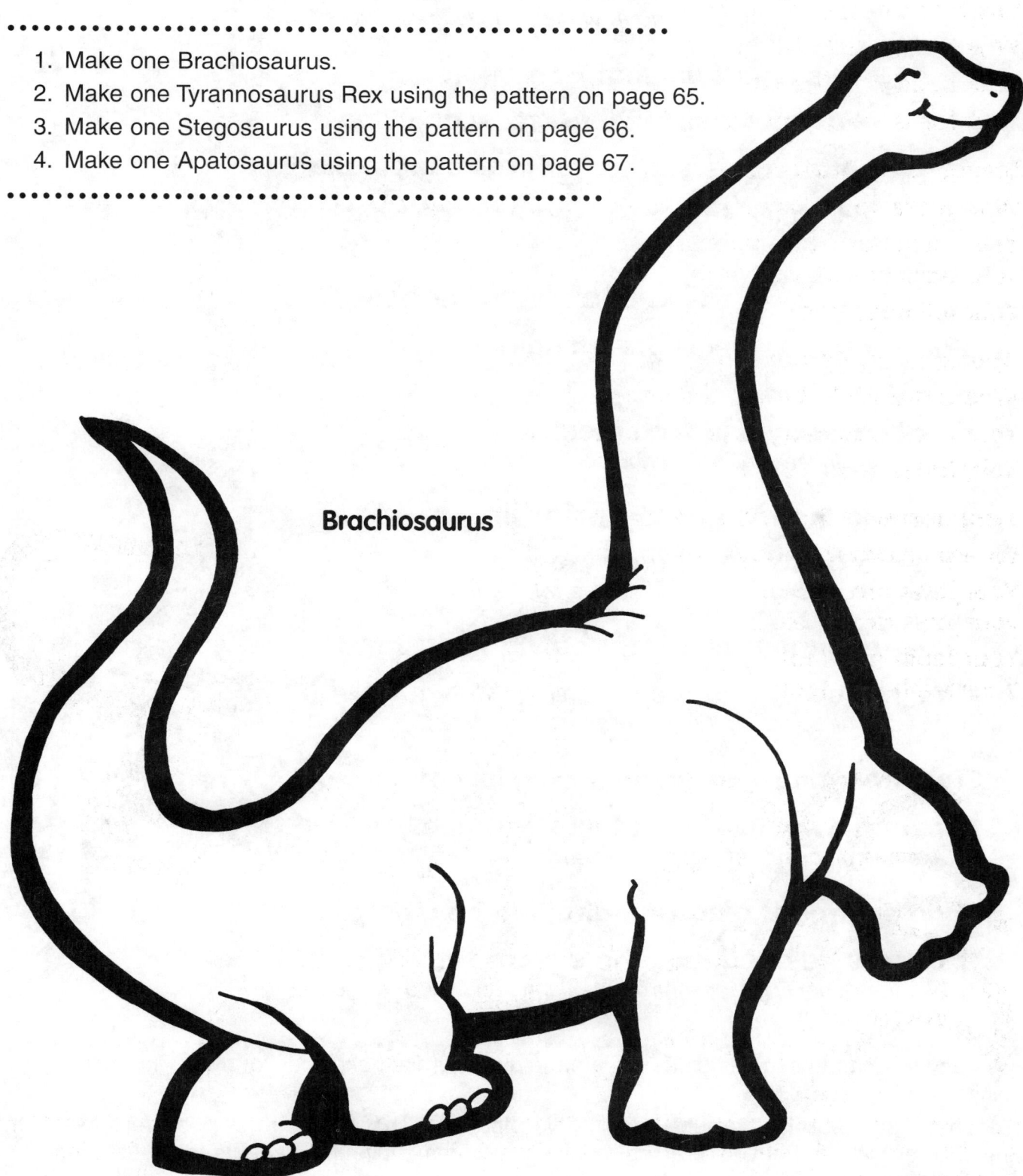

Brachiosaurus

Dinosaur Poems

Five Dinosaurs That I Once Knew
(Sing to the tune of "Five Little Ducks.")

Five dinosaurs that I once knew

Fat ones, skinny ones, scary ones too

But Tyrannosaurus Rex was a great big thing

He ruled the others; he was the King, King, King.

Five Enormous Dinosaurs

Five enormous dinosaurs letting out a roar.
(Place five dinosaurs on the flannelboard.)

One ran away and then there were four.
(Take one dinosaur off the flannelboard.)

Four enormous dinosaurs munching on a tree.

One ran away and then there were three.
(Take one dinosaur off the flannelboard.)

Three enormous dinosaurs eating tiger stew.

One ran away and then there were two.
(Take one dinosaur off the flannelboard.)

Two enormous dinosaurs having lots of fun.

One ran away and then there was one.
(Take one dinosaur off the flannelboard.)

One enormous dinosaur, afraid to be a hero.

He ran away and then there were zero.
(Take the remaining dinosaur off the flannelboard.)

- -

Use any five patterns in this unit to create the dinosaur flannel pieces for "Five Enormous Dinosaurs."

Teacher Suggestion: Share the poem, "Five Dinosaurs That I Once Knew," several times with the children. As part of your reading readiness program, have the students retell the poem using dinosaur stick puppets.

- -

Dinosaur Action Poems

That Enormous Dinosaur

See him come from afar...That enormous dinosaur.
(Create a large round circle with your arms.)

Lumbering, slumbering...Hear the great grumbling.
(Make a loud growling sound.)

Earth shakes, earth quakes...Such a dreadful sound he makes.
(Alternate rocking back and forth from your left to right foot.)

See him come from afar...That enormous dinosaur.
(Cup your hand above your eyes, as if looking far into the distance.)

Eat, Eat, Eat Your Plants

(Sing to the tune of "Row, Row, Row Your Boat.")

Eat, eat, and eat your plants, Mr. Dinosaur.
(Pretend to spoon food into your mouth.)

Hurry up and eat your plants, so you can have some more.
(Quickly move your jaws.)

Dinosaur Moves

Spread your arms, way out wide.
(Reach up with both of your arms spread apart.)

Fly like Pteranodon, soar and glide.
(Pretend to be flying.)

Move like Stegosaurus, long ago.
Bend to the floor, head down low.
(Bend over and swoop down to the floor.)

Reach up tall and try to be,
(Stand on your tiptoes and reach up high.)

A tall Apatosaurus, eating from a tree.
Use your claws, grumble and growl,
(Curl your fingers in front as if growling.)

Just like Tyrannosaurus on the prowl.

Teacher Suggestion: To create flannelboard versions of these poems, use the patterns in this unit to make the dinosaur flannel pieces.

Space Unit

Imagination is critical to young children's development. The space unit provides opportunities to use the flannelboard stories and rhymes as a starting point for discussions that will nourish children's imaginations. Youngsters can take a "trip" in a rocket ship or imagine a spaceman is coming to "visit" their classroom.

Teaching Tip

Make a counting bulletin board. The bulletin board should be low enough so that the children can use it for the activity. Duplicate the rocket ship pattern on page 77 ten times. Label each of the rocket ships with a numeral from 1–10, then add the rocket ships to the bulletin board. Glue a pocket to each of ten blue paper plates. Post a plate under each rocket ship. Place 60 small craft sticks in a container near the display. To complete the counting activity, a child places one stick in the one paper-plate pocket, two in the two pocket, etc.

Art Activity

Let each child make his or her own space satellite using a variety of materials, such as paper towel tubes, small boxes, unused meat trays, and Styrofoam pieces. Allow each child to be creative and decorate his or her satellite using glitter, aluminum foil, tissue paper, or stickers.

Supporting Children with Special Needs

Creating moon balls is a wonderful way to enhance fine motor skills. Have each child make a moon ball by mixing 1 tablespoon honey and 1 tablespoon peanut butter with 2 tablespoons nonfat dry milk in a small bowl. Direct the child to roll the mixture into a ball using the palms of his or her hands. Give each child a small roller and a resealable, plastic bag containing 2 tablespoons of corn flakes. Have him or her use the roller to crush the corn flakes. Then, have the child roll his or her "moon" ball in the crushed corn flakes before eating it.

Teacher Note: Check with the parents of your students to determine if any food allergies exist before beginning this activity. For those students with food allergies, try purchasing some freeze-dried camping food. Explain to students that is it similar to astronaut food.

Enrichment

Demonstrate to the students how a rocket ship works. For this activity you will need ten feet of twine, two large spools, a straw, several long balloons, and masking tape.

First, thread the twine through the straw, tying each end of the twine to one of the spools. Blow up the balloon. (The teacher or assistant holds the balloon and inflates it each time.) Hold the end of the balloon throughout the activity so it won't deflate and tape the balloon to the straw. Direct one child to be the "ground control" and another to be the "flight control." Each child holds one of the spools, pulling slightly so the twine is taut. Ask the flight control child, "Are you brave? You have a scary job." Ask, "Ground control, are you ready? Flight control, are you ready?" Encourage the children to reply, "Ground control is ready," etc. Ask the children who are watching the launch to help with the countdown: 5, 4, 3, 2, 1, 0, blast off. Let go of the balloon. It will travel along the twine to the flight control child. (Many times, the flight control child will drop his or her spool because he or she is surprised that the balloon "rocket" travels so quickly.) Give other children a turn to be in the control positions. Use a new balloon and piece of tape each time you repeat the activity. Discuss with the children how *thrust* propels a balloon or a rocket ship. (The air from inside the balloon/rocket ship, as it is released, forces the balloon/rocket ship to move forward.)

Meeting the Standards: Space Unit

Language Arts

- Asks and answers questions
- Comprehends what others are saying
- Demonstrates competency in speaking as a tool for learning
- Demonstrates competency in listening as a tool for learning
- Follows simple directions
- Identifies and sorts common shape words into basic categories
- Identifies characters, settings, and important events
- Is developing fine motor skills
- Listens
- Produces meaningful linguistic sounds
- Produces rhyming words in response to an oral prompt
- Recites familiar stories and rhymes with patterns
- Recites short stories
- Recognizes meaningful words
- Responds to oral directions
- Responds to oral questions
- Retells familiar stories

Mathematics

- Classifies objects
- Conceptualizes one-to-one correspondence
- Copies and extends patterns
- Counts to ten
- Divides objects into categories
- Implements a problem-solving strategy
- Learns number names and symbols
- Uses verbal communication
- Uses pictorial communication
- Uses symbolic communication
- Understands the problem

Science

- Applies problem-solving skills
- Classifies
- Communicates
- Explores animals
- Identifies objects by properties
- Identifies objects by shape
- Identifies objects by size
- Predicts
- Problem-solves through group activities

Rocket Ship

Rocket ship, rocket ship goes so fast.
(Place the rocket ship on the lower section of the flannelboard.)

Rocket ship, rocket ship, off you blast.
(Move the rocket ship to the upper section of the flannelboard.)

"zh——!" goes the rocket bound for a star.
(Add the star to the flannelboard.)

"zh——!" goes the rocket traveling afar.
Past rainbows, past meteors, past comets at play.
(Add the rainbow, meteor, and comet to the flannelboard.)

The rocket zooms on to a star far away.
"zh——!" goes the rocket bound for a star.
(Start to make your voice softer.)

"zh——!" goes the rocket traveling afar,
"zh————!"
(Carry the last zh longer.)

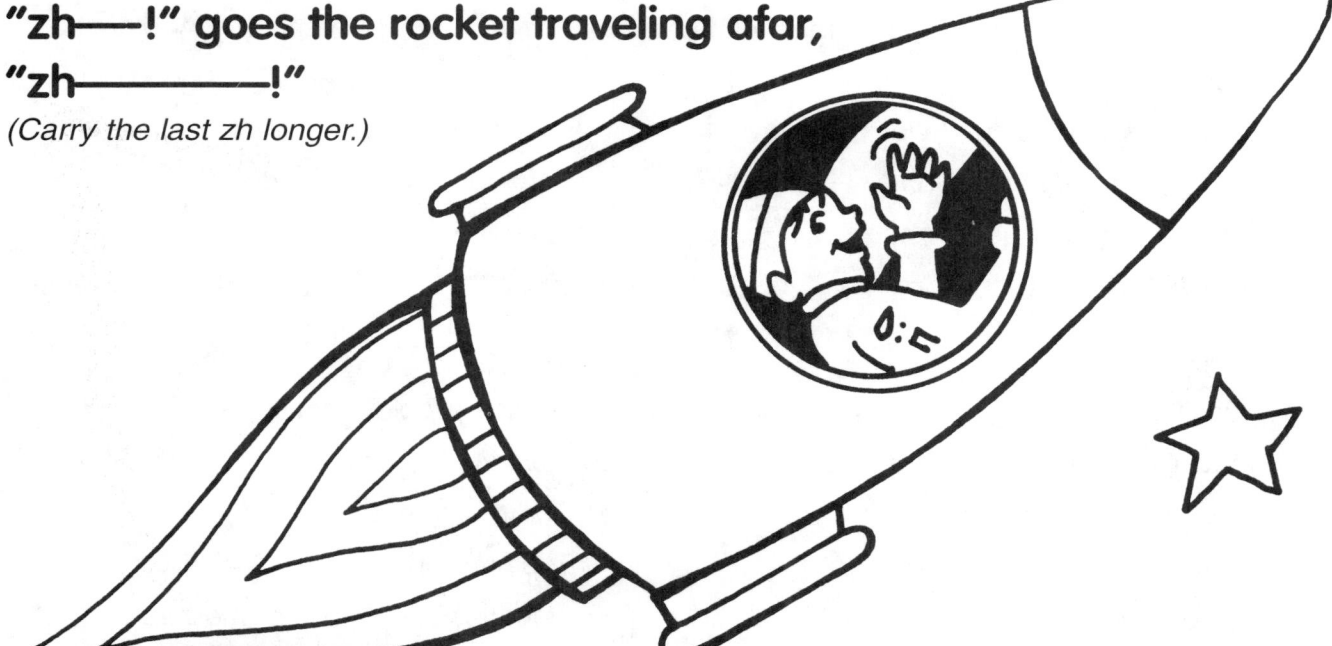

Use the patterns on pages 77–78 to create the rocket ship, rainbow, meteor, star, and comet flannel pieces.

Teacher Suggestion: A short poem, such as "Rocket Ship," can easily be incorporated into your reading readiness curriculum. Display the poem so that it is visible to all the children. Point to each word, as you say it with the children, to introduce the concepts of left-to-right directionality and one-to-one correspondence.

Patterns for Rocket Ship

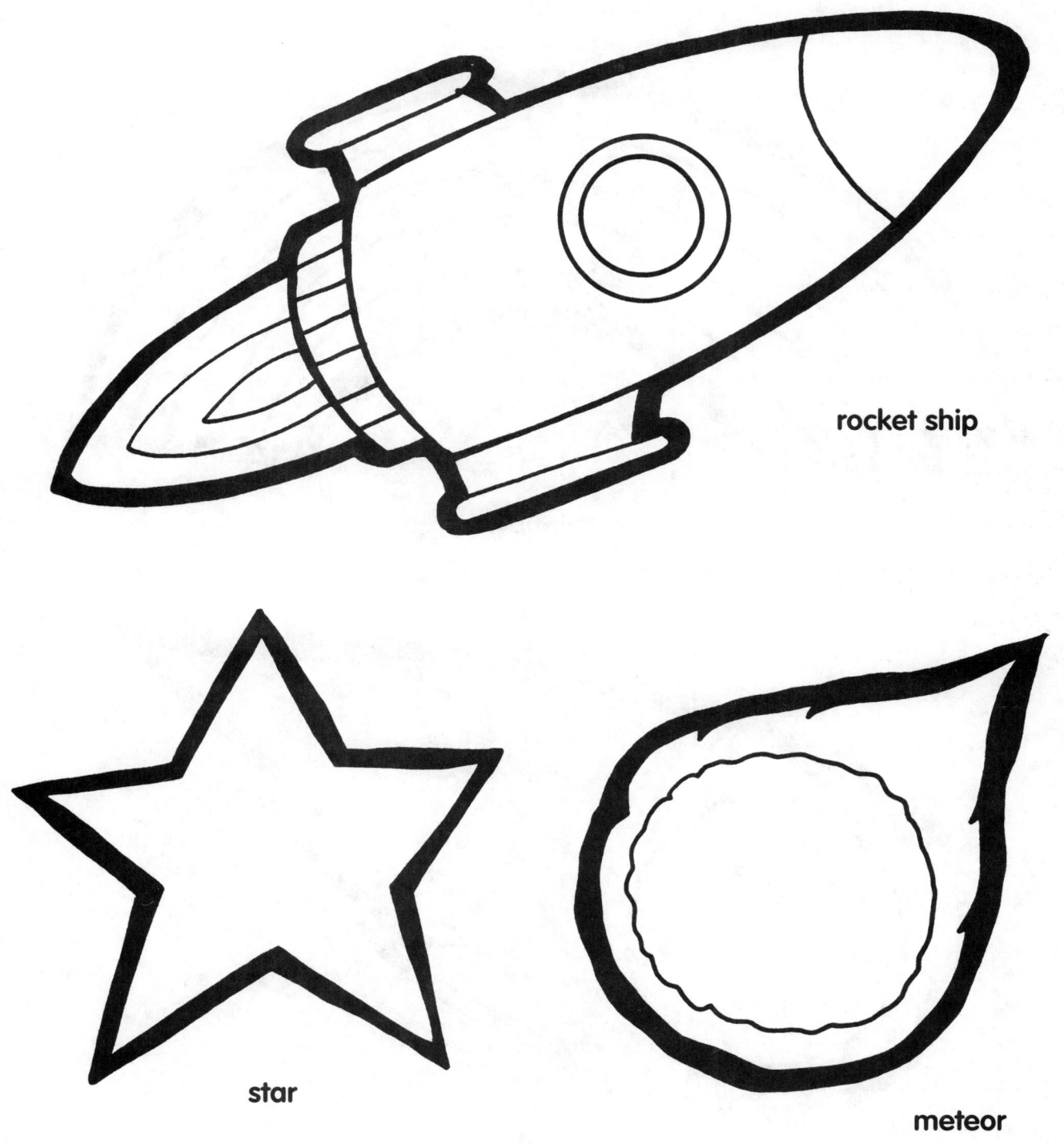

rocket ship

star

meteor

1. Make one rocket ship.
2. Make one star.
3. Make one meteor.

Patterns for Rocket Ship *(cont.)*

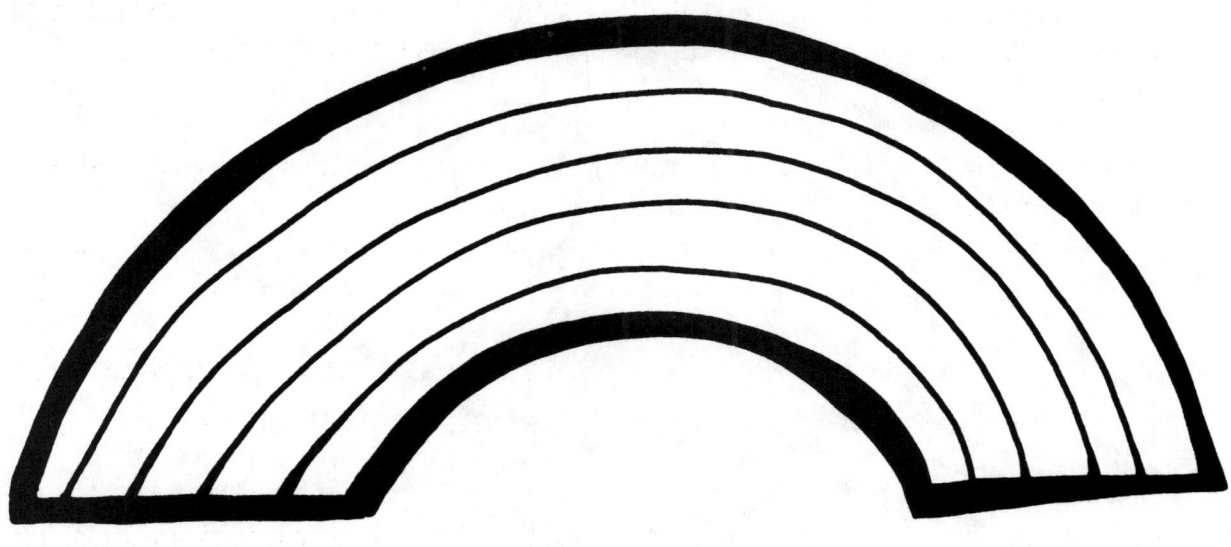

rainbow

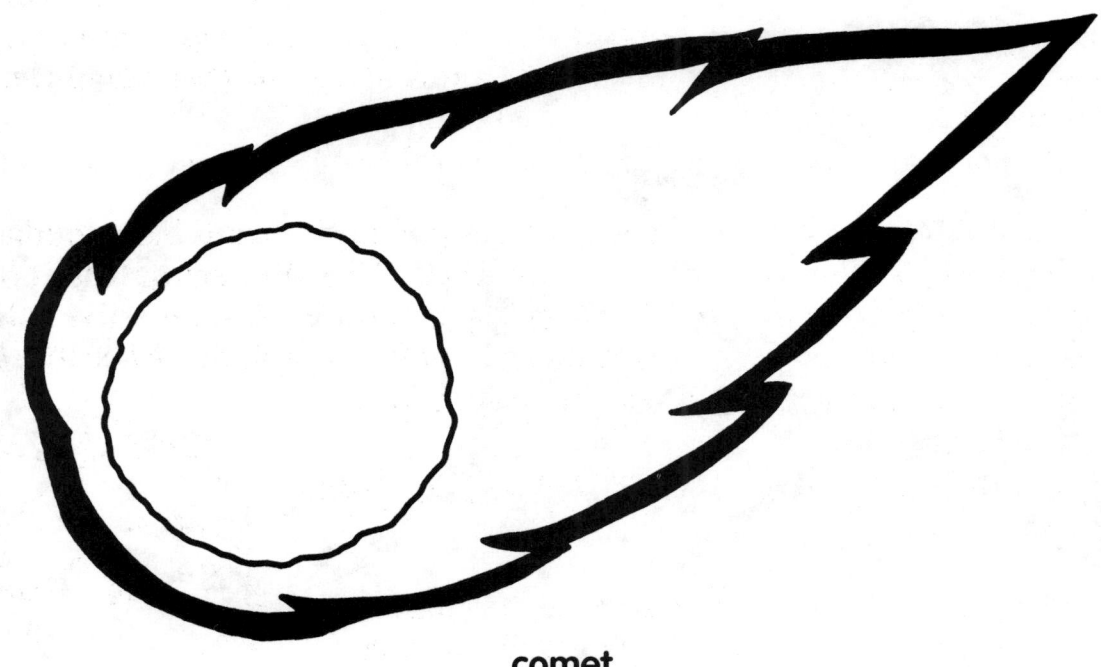

comet

1. Make one rainbow.
2. Make one comet.

The Little Spaceman Who Listened

Do you know what a spaceman is? Maybe most of us don't know what one looks like, but let's make believe, shall we? Let's suppose that he is like a little boy, dressed in bright clothes with a funny looking little hat. Do his clothes look like those you wear? How are they different? Let's call him Sparky.

(Place Sparky on the flannelboard.)

Now, this little spaceman was very special. He had THREE pairs of ears. How many ears would that be?

(Place the three pairs of ears on the flannelboard. Pause for the children to answer the question. If they need prompting, count the ears with the children.)

That's right, that would be SIX ears. They were listening ears. There was a **BIG** pair of ears, a **MEDIUM** pair of ears, and a pair of TINY ears.

(Point to each pair of ears as it is said.)

When Sparky wore his **BIG** pair of ears, he could hear the faintest sounds.

(Put the BIG set of ears on Sparky.)

He heard leaves falling from the trees, the wind whispering to the flowers, and the water rippling over the stones in the little stream. He could hear the dogs barking far away, and he could hear the stars and planets move in the sky. Sparky always told his friends about the dogs and rockets so they could run and hide. They were very thankful.

(Take the BIG ears off the flannelboard and put the TINY ears on Sparky.)

Sparky wore his TINY ears when the storms came and the wind blew loudly and fiercely and when the thunder roared and crashed. The little animals that had only one pair of ears apiece were frightened by the loud noises, but the little spaceman told them that the wind and thunder were important. After those would come the rain, and the rain was important for it made the food grow.

Most of the time Sparky wore his **MEDIUM-SIZED** ears.

(Put the MEDIUM ears on Sparky.)

He liked them best of all. He listened to all the medium-sized sounds with them. Not the very loud and not the very soft sounds, but the sounds that are nice to listen to.

One morning, some children came to the woods to pick flowers. *(Put the flowers on the flannelboard.)*

The Little Spaceman Who Listened *(cont.)*

"What should we do with the flowers?" a little girl asked.

A boy named Billy said, "Let's take them to school." "Yes, let's," said one of the girls. "We can show them to the children at sharing time."

Sparky listened and wished that he could go to school. He wanted to see and hear what the children did at sharing time. He told his friends about it, but they said, "No, a spaceman cannot go to school. School is for children." But Sparky decided to go to school anyway. So the next morning, he crept out of his little spaceship where he had hidden and zoomed up into the air and down into the schoolhouse.

(Place the schoolhouse and Sparky on his rocket on the flannelboard.)

He found the schoolhouse by following the children as they walked to school. He landed up in a tree and watched the children playing out on the school ground.

(Place the tree on the flannelboard. Put Sparky and his rocket on the tree.)

Just then, the bell rang and the children all went inside.

If Sparky were here in our classroom, which pair of ears do you think he would have to use? Would he use his **BIG** ears because you talk low? Would he use his **TINY** ears because you talk too loud, or his **MEDIUM** ears because you are talking just right—loud enough for everyone to hear but not shouting. Remember, Sparky likes his **MEDIUM** ears best!

• •

Use the patterns on pages 81, 82, 83, and 91 to create the Sparky, ears, flowers, schoolhouse, tree, and Sparky-on-his-rocket flannel pieces.

• •

Patterns for The Little Spaceman
Who Listened

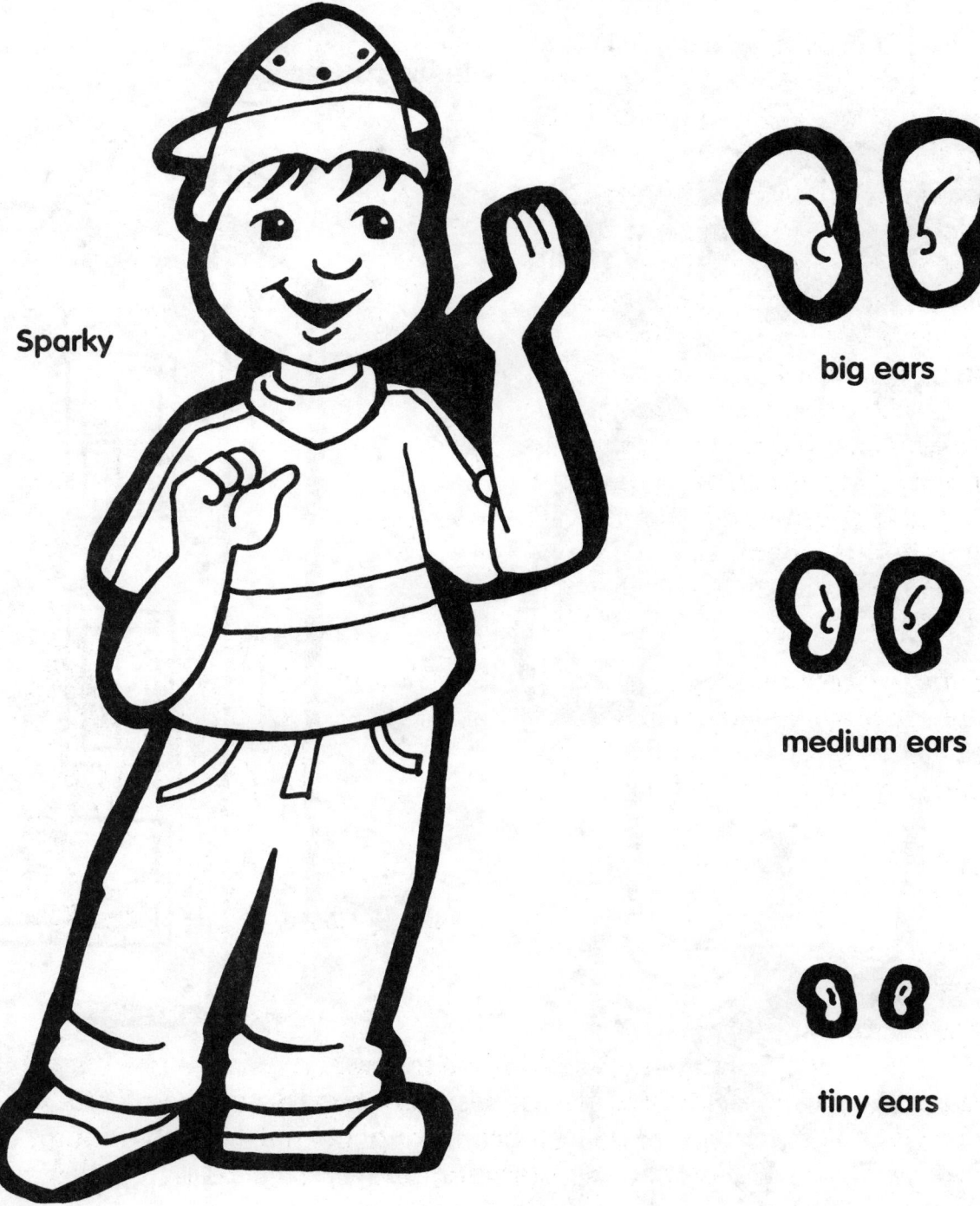

Sparky

big ears

medium ears

tiny ears

1. Make one Sparky without his spacesuit.
2. Make one pair of big ears.
3. Make one pair of medium ears.
4. Make one pair of tiny ears.

Patterns for The Little Spaceman Who Listened *(cont.)*

Sparky in his spacesuit

schoolhouse

1. Make one Sparky in his spacesuit.
2. Make one schoolhouse. (Enlarge the schoolhouse if possible.)

Patterns for The Little Spaceman
Who Listened *(cont.)*

Sparky on his rocket

wildflower bouquet

1. Make one Sparky on his rocket.
2. Make one bouquet of wildflowers.
3. Make one tree using the pattern on page 91. Enlarge the pattern if possible.

Nine Little Planets

One little, two little, three little planets.

Four little, five little, six little planets.

Seven little, eight little, nine little planets.

In our great big solar system.

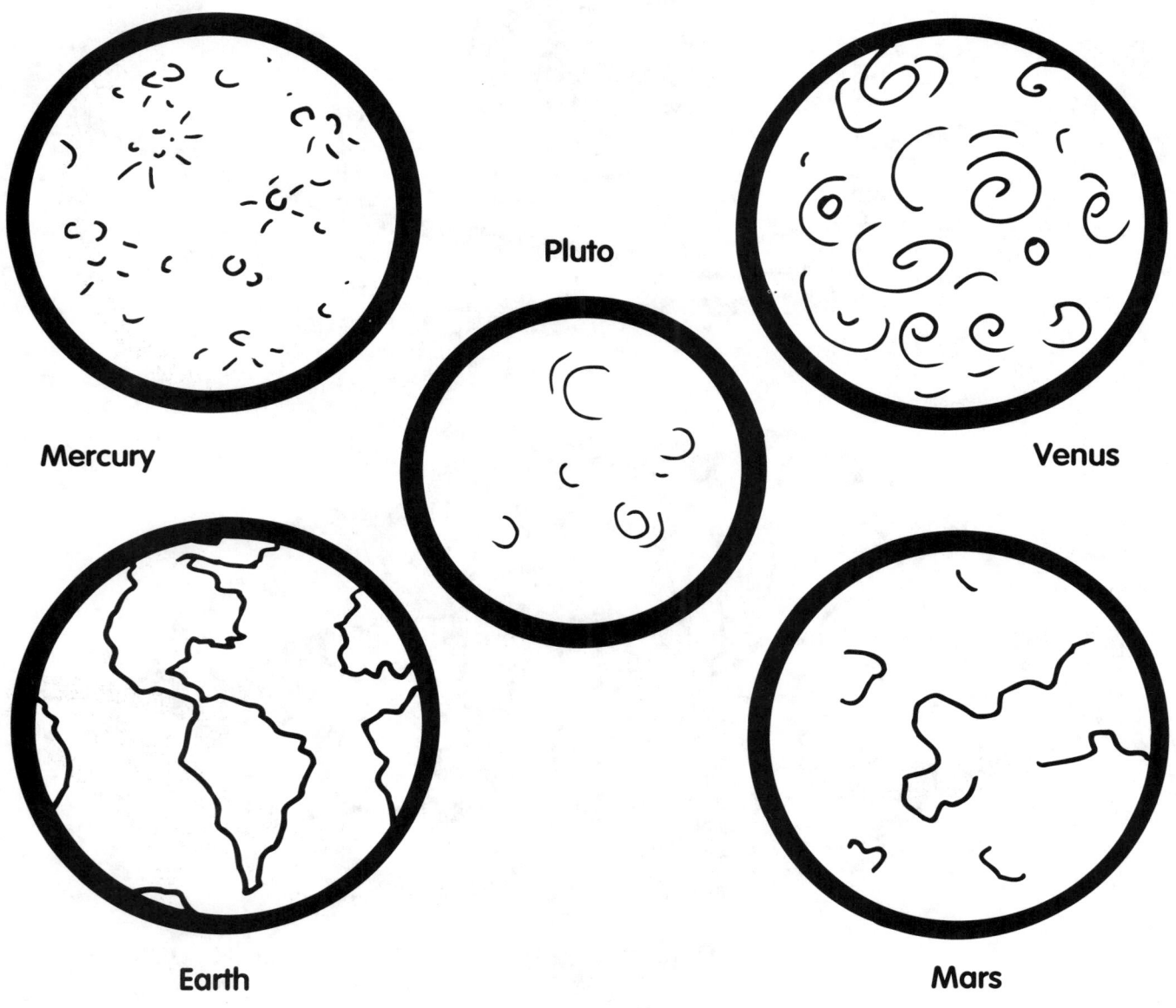

Use the patterns above and on page 85 to create Mercury, Venus, Earth, Mars, Jupiter, Uranus, Neptune, Saturn, and Pluto stick puppets. Choose appropriate colors for each.

Patterns for Nine Little Planets

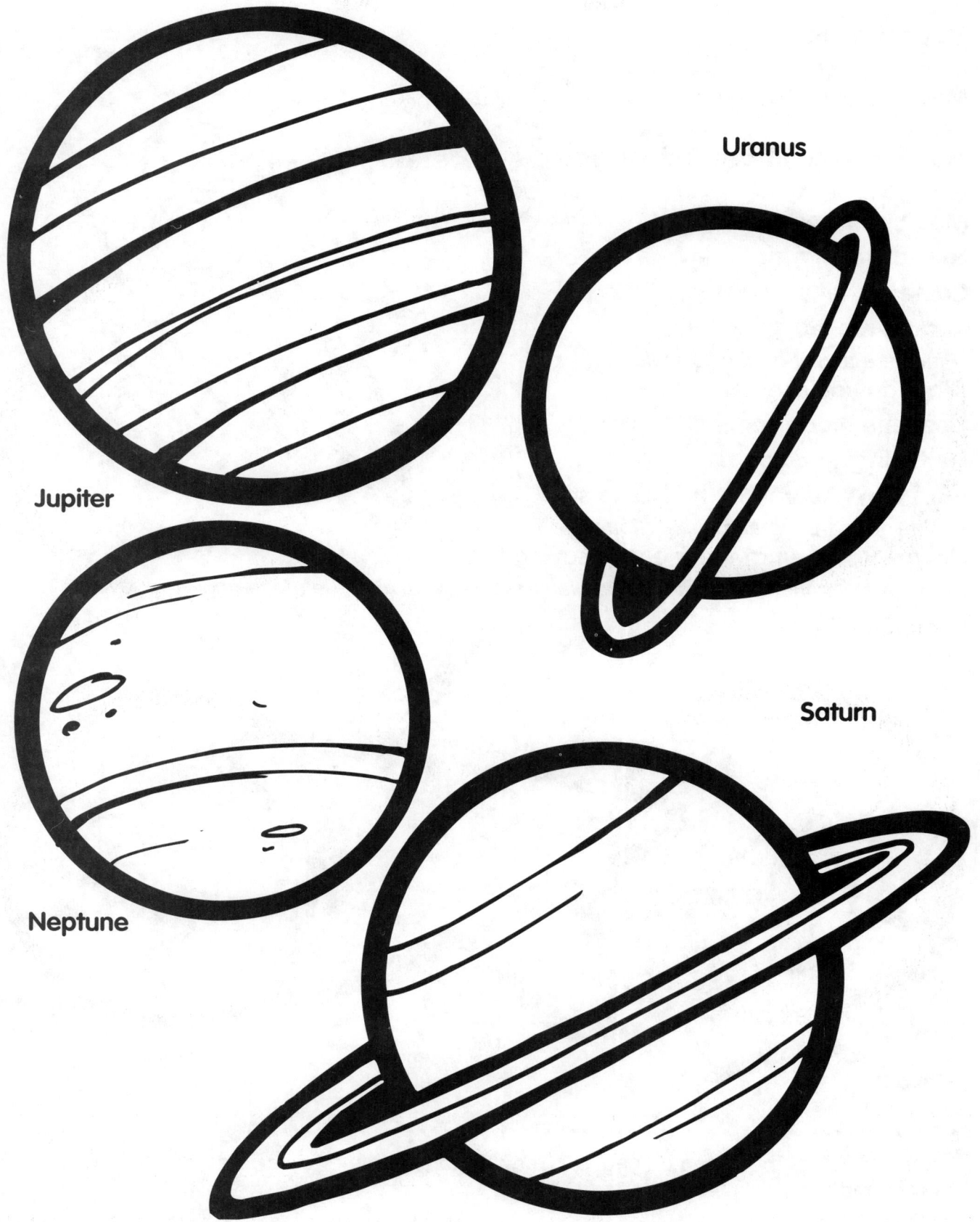

Uranus

Jupiter

Saturn

Neptune

Moon, Sing Me a Song

Moon, sing me a song.
(Place the moon on the flannelboard.)
Moon, look at the stars.
(Place the stars on the flannelboard.)
Moon, how can I can find Mars?
(Place a large question mark on the flannelboard.)
Moon, sing me a song.
Let's all take a trip today.
Come on, let's fly away.
Rocket, rocket, flying by.
(Place the rocket on the flannelboard.)
What do you see in the sky?
I see the moon coming this way.
He is singing a song.
But I can't hear what he has to say.
(Hold your hand up and cup it around your ear.)
Do you know what the moon is saying?
(Ask the children to use their imaginations and tell you what the moon might be saying.)

stars

Use the patterns above and on pages 77 and 87 to create the rocket, star, moon, and large question mark flannel pieces.

Patterns for Moon, Sing Me a Song

moon

question mark

1. Make one moon.
2. Make one question mark.
3. Make one rocket using the pattern on page 77.
4. Make three stars using the patterns on page 86.

Space Helmet

Put on your space helmet.
(Pretend to strap on a helmet.)

Put on your spacesuit.
(Pretend to step into a spacesuit and zip it.)

Strap an oxygen tank to your back.
(Pat your back as if strapping on the oxygen tank.)

We'll all take a trip on a rocket ship
All the way to the moon and back!
Five, four, three, two, one, zero!

Blast off!
(Get low to the ground and jump up as you "blast off.")

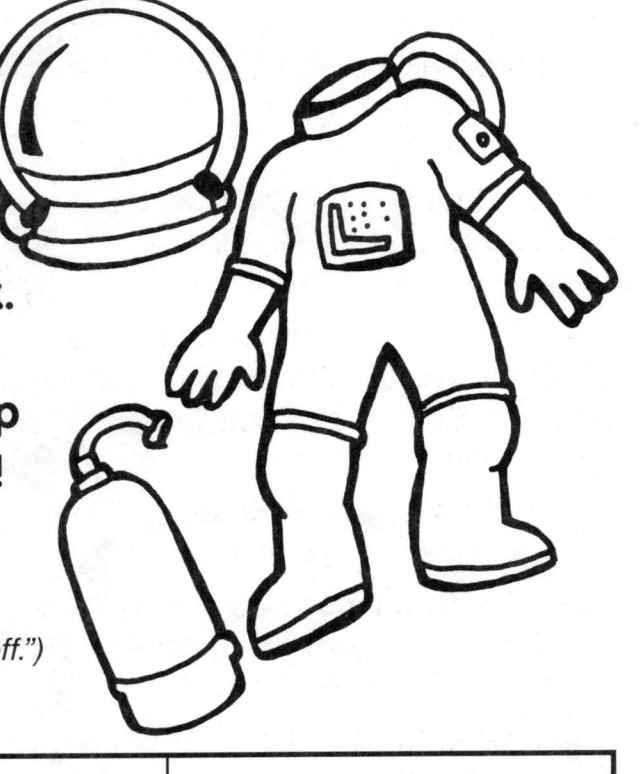

0	1	2
3	4	5

Enlarge numeral cards above for counting down. Line up six children holding the numeral cards. Have each child sit down as his or her number is said.

Sleepy Mr. Sun

Mr. Sun opened one eye and peeked out over the top of the meadow. He saw Mr. Moon dropping out of sight at the other end of the meadow, so he knew it was time to get up.
(Put both Mr. Sun and Mr. Moon on the flannelboard. Add a few stars.)

But Mr. Sun was still sleepy. He covered his face with a cloud blanket and decided to go back to sleep.
(Place the cloud on the flannelboard, covering most of Mr. Sun.)

Then Mr. Sun began to think. If I do not get up, who is going to brush the dew off the flowers? Who is going to make warm sunshine for the boys and girls to play in? So he threw off the cloud and rose in the sky.
(Lift the sun above the cloud. Take Mr. Moon off the flannelboard.)

As he did this, the robin in the tree sang her pretty good morning song.
(Put the robin in a tree on the flannelboard.)

Now, Mr. Sun was wide awake. He climbed high in the sky, looking for his breakfast. He gobbled up a few stars left over from the evening before.
(Take the stars off the flannelboard.)

He worked hard to bring bright sunshine for the children as they walked to school and for the plants to grow strong. In the evening, when he was tired again, he pulled back the cloud cover and closed his eyes.
(Put the cloud back over the sun. Place Mr. Moon on the flannelboard.)

"Good night, world," said Mr. Sun. And he went fast asleep.

cloud

Use the patterns above and on pages 86, 90, and 91 to create the stars, cloud, Mr. Sun, Mr. Moon, robin in a tree, and plants flannel pieces.

1. Make one cloud.

Space

Patterns for Sleepy Mr. Sun

Mr. Moon

Mr. Sun

1. Make one Mr. Sun.
2. Make one Mr. Moon.
3. Make several stars using the patterns on page 86.
4. Make one cloud using the pattern on page 89.

Patterns for Sleepy Mr. Sun (cont.)

robin in a tree

plants

1. Make several plants.
2. Make one robin in a tree. (Enlarge this pattern if possible.)

The Sky Is Full of Clouds

This little cloud likes to laugh and play.

This little cloud does tricks all day.

This little cloud makes a great big frown.

This little cloud turns upside down.

This little cloud rolls like a ball.

This little cloud is very tall.

And this little cloud is the shape of a tree.

My, my, this little cloud looks like me!

frowning cloud

laughing cloud

tricky cloud

Enlarge the patterns above and on page 93 to create cloud stick puppets. Use these puppets to illustrate each line of text.

1. Make two laughing clouds. Use one for the upside-down cloud.
2. Make one tricky cloud.
3. Make one frowning cloud.

Patterns for The Sky Is Full of Clouds

ball cloud

tall cloud

tree cloud

eyes-wide-open cloud

1. Make one ball cloud.
2. Make one tall cloud.

3. Make one tree cloud.
4. Make one cloud with eyes wide open.

Ten Little Martians

Ten little martians standing in a row.
(Have ten children stand in a row.)

When they see the captain they salute just so.
(Extend hand from forehead to form a salute.)

They march to the left,
(March to the left.)

And they march to the right.
(March to the right.)

Then they close their eyes, and sleep all night.
(Close your eyes and fold your hands as if you are falling asleep.)

Enlarge the numerical cards above and on page 88. Select ten students to hold the cards in numerical order. After saying the second line of the poem, have each student stand up, in turn, and say his or her number to reinforce counting skills.

Space Poems

Ring Around the Rocket Ship

(Sing to the tune of "Ring Around the Rosy.")

Ring around the rocket ship.
Try to grab a star.
Stardust, stardust.
Fall where you are.

I See the Moon

I see the moon.
The moon sees me.
The moon sees someone it wants to see.
Now whom does the moon see?
(Use a mirror to shine on the face of a child.)

The moon sees _____.
(Fill in the name of the child.)

It's a Very Special World

(Sing to the tune of "It's a Small World.")

It's a world of sun and a world of night.
There are planets, moons, and starlight.
If we open our eyes,
It's a world of surprise.
It's a special world after all.
It's a special world after all.
It's a special world after all.
It's a very special world.

•••

Teacher Suggestion: Use the patterns on pages 77, 84–87, and 96 to create rocket ship, star, stardust, moon, sun, and planet stick puppets.

•••

Patterns for Space Poems

sun

moon

stardust

1. Make some stardust for "Ring Around the Rocket Ship."
2. Make one winking moon for "I See the Moon."
3. Make one sun for "It's a Very Special World."
4. Make one rocket ship using the pattern on page 77 for "Ring Around the Rocket Ship."
5. Make one star using the pattern on page 77 for "Ring Around the Rocket Ship."
6. Make one set of planets using the patterns on pages 84–85 for "It's a Very Special World."
7. Make several moons using the pattern on page 87 for "It's a Very Special World."
8. Make several stars using the patterns on page 86 for "It's a Very Special World."